The Careerist

The Careerist
Over 100 ways to get ahead at work

RHYMER RIGBY

KoganPage

LONDON   PHILADELPHIA   NEW DELHI

First published in Great Britain and the United States in 2012 by Kogan Page Limited

Apart from any fair dealing for the purposes of research or private study, or criticism or review, as permitted under the Copyright, Designs and Patents Act 1988, this publication may only be reproduced, stored or transmitted, in any form or by any means, with the prior permission in writing of the publishers, or in the case of reprographic reproduction in accordance with the terms and licences issued by the CLA. Enquiries concerning reproduction outside these terms should be sent to the publishers at the undermentioned addresses:

120 Pentonville Road	1518 Walnut Street, Suite 1100	4737/23 Ansari Road
London N1 9JN	Philadelphia PA 19102	Daryaganj
United Kingdom	USA	New Delhi 110002
www.koganpage.com		India

© Rhymer Rigby, 2012

The right of Rhymer Rigby to be identified as the author of this work has been asserted by him in accordance with the Copyright, Designs and Patents Act 1988.

ISBN   978 0 7494 6592 6
E-ISBN   978 0 7494 6593 3

British Library Cataloguing-in-Publication Data

A CIP record for this book is available from the British Library.

Library of Congress Cataloging-in-Publication Data

Rigby, Rhymer.
    The careerist : Over 100 ways to get ahead at work / Rhymer Rigby.
        p. cm.
    Includes bibliographical references.
    ISBN 978-0-7494-6592-6 – ISBN 978-0-7494-6593-3   1. Career development.
2. Success in business.   I. Title.
    HF5381.R624 2012
    650.14–dc23
                                                            2012015758

Typeset by Graphicraft Limited, Hong Kong
Print production managed by Jellyfish
Printed and bound by CPI Group (UK) Ltd, Croydon, CR0 4YY

Contents

Acknowledgements

I'd like to thank all the people who spoke to me, many on several occasions, for 'The Careerist' columns in the *Financial Times* and whose expertise makes this book what it is.

I'd also like to thank the Business Life team at the *Financial Times* – Ravi Mattu, Harriet Arnold and Emma Jacobs. Most of all, though, I'd like to thank Gautam Malkani at the *FT* who edited these columns – and in virtually all cases improved on the original.

Finally, I'd like to thank my agent, Simon Benham.

Introduction

When you look at writing a weekly column based around a single subject area, one of the first considerations, before you all agree it's a goer, is whether you can easily come up with, say, 25 topics or about six months' worth of slots. With 'The Careerist', the *FT*'s Business Life team and I did this and agreed that six months down the line we'd see how things were going. That was over two years ago and, even now, when I realistically expected to be scraping the bottom of the barrel, I rarely sit around agonizing over what I'm going to write about next week. I had hugely underestimated the natural stock of resources to be found in office life.

With the benefit of hindsight, this was perhaps obvious for a number of reasons. First, most people spend eight hours a day or more at work. More time than they spend with their families, more time than they spend asleep. Selling our time to an employer is, for most of us, our single most significant activity. Not only that, but work is taking up more of our lives, not less. Second, one of the biggest points of work is getting ahead, whether it's for straight-forward reasons (you want to become CEO) or secondary reasons (you want a bigger house). Third, there are innumerable routes, if not to the very top, then at least upwards. And fourth, not everyone behaves well (as the career coach Blaire Palmer says in the piece in this book dealing with favouritism, 'We expect organizations to be like a family but they're often more like the playground'). These are just a few reasons and there are doubtless dozens more – the thing about the workplace is that all human life is there.

The upshot of this is that most of us deal with dozens of issues and situations every week that could have a bearing on our careers. Some of them are seemingly trivial – using humour in the office, drinks with colleagues or going on holiday properly. Others are more obviously serious – sacking someone, commanding respect and coming back from your own failures. Some are even strangely abstract such as becoming an iconoclast. What they all share, though, is that, large or small, they offer opportunities to shine or, at the very least, minimize the career damage you suffer when things go wrong. Moreover, in many of these situations the way forward is not entirely obvious and there are plenty of tips and tricks that help you come out ahead.

Perhaps unsurprisingly one of the most enjoyable things about writing this column has been doing the 300-plus interviews that went into this book. Many are with the kind of people you'd expect – career coaches, business psychologists, headhunters, academics and so on. But others are a little more out there. For instance, there is Robin Jay, America's foremost expert on the art of business lunch. There is William Hanson, a well known etiquette consultant. There is Joe Navarro, a former FBI agent who's a globally renowned expert on body language. And there's Gerald Ratner, the man who memorably called his products crap – on how to bounce back from failure. I am indebted to all these experts who have been kind enough to speak to me over the last two years and let me pick their brains.

As the number of experts whose careers are in areas as diverse as leadership development, personal branding and personal organization doubtless points up, I am not an expert on any single area. And the point of this book is not to provide an exhaustive answer on how to manage under-performers, set career goals or even do a business breakfast. If you look on Amazon or on the business shelves of your local bookstore, you'll find whole books devoted to many of the topics which this book covers in 650 words – and quite a few of them will have been written by people quoted in this book.

What this book is intended to offer, though, is a kind of gazetteer to the world of work. Worried about making a good first impression or how to conduct an interview? Well, here are the basics. Need to ask someone for help or think you've chosen the wrong job? Here are half a dozen pointers. Realize you don't know how to sack someone or ask for a pay rise? This will provide you with a good grounding. The advice is pithy, useful, to the point and any of the topics can be read in under five minutes. That should be enough to recommend it to anyone who wants to get ahead at work.

Chapter One
Moving onwards and upwards

Dealing with a blot on your CV

Many people have something in their working past that they would rather potential employers didn't know about. But how do you minimize the impact of a black mark on your CV?

What constitutes a blot on my résumé?

There is a whole spectrum, from the very trivial to the very serious. 'There's quite a difference between something very serious like fraud or professional misconduct and the guilt-by-association type stuff where you've been working for a company that's collapsed,' says Janet Moran, managing director of the CV House. 'If it's the latter, it's entirely possible to move on easily.'

How should I play it?

'Your CV needs to be a fair and accurate representation of you – and if it isn't, you can be dismissed, so you must never lie,' says Nigel Parslow, UK managing director of the executive search firm Harvey Nash. 'But a CV is also a marketing tool, so you can expand on the good points and gloss over the bad ones.'

Corinne Mills, managing director of Personal Career Management, says: 'It amazes me how many people draw attention to their shortcomings. They seem to want to announce them out loud. People often supply way too much information.'

Examples of this include mentioning that you were made redundant after working somewhere for years or detailing a decades-old poor degree result. But if you are asked about something you've glossed over in an interview, you should play it straight.

'Work out the question you would least like to be asked and practise answering it until you have a plausible response that you can deliver confidently,' says Miranda Kennett of First Class Coach.

Are all negative experiences negative?

'Candidates' perceptions of these blots can be far worse than they are,' says Ms Moran. 'People who've been through tough times are often more useful and experienced than those who've only had things go well for them.'

When it comes to negative experiences, time is a great amnesiac. 'If you're in your 50s, no one cares about how you messed around in your early 20s,' says Mr Parslow. However, he says multiple blots are harder to dismiss: 'Everyone can make one mistake, but if you have two in a row, it starts to look like the problem is you.'

What about illness?

Ms Mills says that many people feel the compulsion to detail every-thing about their health, even when it isn't asked for. 'Especially if it is something that's been resolved, you should take the view that if you're going for the job you're fit to do it and that's that.' However, she adds, long periods of illness may need to be explained. 'In this case, write a covering letter, stressing that it's in your past and that you are completely recovered now.'

What if my blot is especially glaring or recent?

'If you have a big, recent gap or issue, you might do a functional CV, which lists your skills and experience on the first page, rather than a chronological one,' says Ms Mills.

If things are really bad, however, moving on may be tougher. Ms Moran suggests looking at different industries, using career transition companies and leveraging the power of your network. 'If you have messed up very badly, you could ask people you know and who are trusted and have professional standing to vouch for you.'

How to write a covering letter

A covering letter is often still regarded as a proforma adjunct to a CV. This is a mistake many people make and taking this attitude could mean that your CV does not get read.

Why are covering letters important?

Your covering letter is likely to be the first thing any prospective employer sees of you. 'It's important to stand out from the crowd and a well thought-out covering letter can make the difference between being shortlisted and being dropped,' says Clive Davis, a director at financial recruitment consultancy Robert Half. 'The whole point of the covering letter is to get you the interview.'

What points should I make?

Your letter should target the job you are applying for. 'You need to remember that at the forefront of the reader's mind is the question: Why should I employ this person?' says business writing consultant Stephen Lloyd. 'Give them reasons. Summarize why you should be interviewed. It needs to be a sales letter.'

James Phillips, a senior adviser at The Fuller CV, adds: 'It is very important to do some research on the company and the role and how you meet their requirements.'

Mr Davis suggests you give examples of projects where you have added value for employers and link your experiences to the role being advertised. It is fine to mention your interests and show a bit of your personality too, but this should not be a main point.

What about style?

The last thing you want to do is sound like everyone else. 'Your letter should sound individually crafted and fresh,' says Mr Lloyd. 'Don't use a common letter for all applications and don't copy sample letters off the internet.'

He adds that your letter will also provide the first example an employer will see of your communication skills. 'Your covering letter doesn't just support your CV, it also shows how you communicate. It needs to be clear, accurate, well written, and the tone needs to be appropriate.'

How long should it be?

Brevity is a must as employers are unlikely to devote much time to to first-round applications. 'It should be no more than one page and there should be a fair amount of white space,' says Mr Phillips. Mr Davis advises: 'If anything takes too long to explain, just leave it out.'

What should I avoid?

'Try and stay away from clichés such as "I'm a team player" and "I have a lot to offer",' says Mr Lloyd. 'They mean very little and don't differentiate you.'

He also warns against relying entirely on spellchecks. 'They won't pick up subtle mistakes like *principle* and *principal* and *form* and *from*.'

You should not mention negatives unless asked about them. 'Avoid humour and being cute,' adds Mr Davis. 'You can often get away with cleverness verbally, by using the right tone of voice and body language. But you won't be there when your letter is read.'

What if I'm applying online?

The letter should be essentially the same. '[However], with a covering e-mail, a lot of companies use sophisticated software to search for key words,' warns Mr Davis. 'So use words relevant to the job and mention them more than once.'

How to be interviewed

Professionals can sometimes be a little blasé about preparing for an interview and developing their technique, believing their CVs and accomplishments speak for themselves. But in today's cut-throat job market, there is little room for complacency.

How do I prepare?

You should research the company beforehand but many people don't, says London-based interview coach Margaret Buj. 'It's very rare that someone has a thorough understanding of the company even at the £100,000–£150,000 level. You need to do more than just read the website. Look at the annual report, press releases and cuttings. Go in with unexpected information – that'll really make you stand out.'

Nick Smallman, managing director of Working Voices, a communications skills consultancy, adds: 'You need to get together a list of tight good-to-go speeches that you can deliver with confidence.'

How should I structure my answers during the interview?

'It helps if you think about three overlapping circles,' says Ceri Roderick, author of *You're Hired!* and a partner at occupational psychologists Pearn Kandola. 'The first is task-focused – how do you get stuff done and deliver? The second is about thought leadership – how do you inspire, are you creative? And the third is about people management.'

Give the interviewer what they ask for. 'If it's a task question, don't start waffling about people. And, above all, root your answers in concrete examples,' he adds.

Ms Buj agrees: 'People give generic overviews but what interviewers really want are specific examples of what you've done and how they relate to the job description. That's what makes you memorable.'

You also want to have a few decent questions of your own to ask and, when it is time to go, show gratitude and tell them you want the job. 'Leave them feeling better than when you came in,' says Mr Smallman.

How do I improve my presentation and delivery?

'Make sure you're rested and focused,' says Mr Smallman. 'Don't rush to your interview. During the interview, you should aim to build a rapport. Connect on a human level and add value. But don't overdo it. Don't just talk about yourself and don't be too verbose. Show modesty and be a good listener.'

In terms of body language, he advises: 'Sit up and be open. Keep your face switched on and smile. You need to be in the moment. If there's more than one person in the interview, make sure you look at everyone.'

How do I deal with difficult questions?

When discussing your weaknesses, Mr Roderick says: 'You should acknowledge them and say you manage them. Be as honest as is sensible.'

That said, he adds that most middle to senior management interviews are not adversarial. 'Go in with the right attitude – that it's a discussion about a job,' he says. 'The idea is not to make you look foolish or put you on the spot.'

Mr Smallman says that you shouldn't worry too much if you're not getting on like old friends. 'It doesn't mean things are going badly – look for what interests them, but remember not every interviewer is the life of the party.'

What to do if you've chosen the wrong job

You have started in a new job, but soon realize it is not the right position for you. What should you do next – and how do you minimize the negative consequences for all concerned?

Where do I start?

This is probably quite a complex situation. 'Work out what is wrong and get some support,' says Jane Barrett, an executive coach and co-author of *If Not Now, When? How to Take Charge of Your Career*.

Fraser Smart, UK managing director of human resources specialist Buck Consultants, says: 'You should give both sides a chance to see if [the situation] can be recovered.'

Should I stay...?

'If you have messed around in the past with numerous short stints, it may be worth staying longer,' says Ruth Colling, a director at business psychologists Nicholson McBride. 'Spending a year somewhere can look like a strategic move. You need to evaluate what it is that is not right and work out whether you can influence or change these things.'

She adds: 'You may also hate a new job simply because it takes you out of your comfort zone – but that is a benefit.'

Ms Barrett says: 'Finding a new job can take months. Stay where you are and keep the money coming in. If you already have a job, you look less desperate in interviews.'

...or should I go?

If your role has a high profile, it can be more noticeable and therefore more damaging to stay on for several months before finally giving up, says Ms Colling. Also, a quick exit before any probationary period ends is a lot easier.

Other reasons for leaving sooner rather than later include if the problems concern things that cannot be changed, such as the company culture. Or you may hate the job so much it makes you ill. 'You have to put your sanity and well-being first,' says Ms Barrett.

If you act fast, as Mr Smart points out, 'You may be able to reconsider other jobs you were looking at during your search.'

How can I improve matters?

'Ask for good, clear feedback,' says Ms Barrett. 'Try to analyse what is wrong.' Ms Colling suggests talking to someone neutral about your predicament and, if appropriate, your manager.

Remember that the new employer will have invested time and money in recruiting you and is likely to want to help. It may turn out that small changes make a huge difference. Mr Smart says: 'If it is a large business, you may also want to look at different areas within the company. You could ask for an extension of your probationary period.'

How do I explain a short stint to other employers?

'Everyone is allowed to make one bad job choice,' says Mr Smart. 'Tell prospective employers.'

However, if you have form in this, you may wish to consider contracting, consultancy or setting up a business before looking for another long-term position in order to put some distance between the job that did not work out and applying for new jobs.

Finally, you may not be required to explain anything: 'If your job lasted less than a month, it may not be picked up by new employers.'

A better job offer

You have accepted one job offer but then a better one comes along. It is a nice problem to have but that does not make it any less of a dilemma.

What should I take into account?

'You need to think quite hard about what constitutes a better offer, especially if you've gone through a recruitment process for a senior role,' says Alan Redman, a business psychologist with the Criterion Partnership. 'Make sure you ask yourself if the new offer is as good a fit. This is particularly true if the better offer is financially better. Once you're in a role, salary tends to be unimportant compared to things like your relationship with your boss.'

Corinne Mills, joint managing director of Personal Career Management, advises: 'If you're unsure, go and spend half a day in the new company. You'll pick up very quickly on whether it's right for you.'

You should also bear in mind that the first company may counter-offer. If you are using the second company's offer as a negotiating chip that's fine, but you shouldn't get into negotiations if you already know you're going to go for the second job.

Does it depend on where I am in the process?

As the old joke has it, verbal agreements are not worth the paper they're written on – and the verbal agreement stage is perhaps the last point at which you can walk away without much awkwardness. This is also true of the better offer. 'The first thing is to make sure you have the better offer in writing,' says Ms Mills. 'Until that happens, you shouldn't say anything.' If you haven't signed and think that a better offer is likely, you may need to delay a bit. It is perfectly OK to say you need time to look at the contract, but Nigel Parslow, UK managing director of Harvey Nash Executive Search, says: 'You need to manage the process professionally and if you're unsure, it's better to stay silent until you're sure.'

What if I have signed a contract?

'Here, you're contractually engaged,' says Mr Parslow. 'To cut and run is a bit cheap really and it eats at your integrity.'

Ms Mills says you need to do what is right for your career, though she adds: 'If you've signed, then legally you do need to be a bit careful. It might be worth getting the contract checked out by a lawyer. However, although HR departments can take legal action against you, they rarely do. They'll normally write it off. If you don't want to be there, they'd rather you weren't there.'

How do I deal with actually letting them down?

Mr Redman says the way you tell them should be appropriate to the relationship that's been formed.

'If you've been in regular telephone contact then this is how you should tell them. Anything else is cowardly. Tell them what attracted you to their job and be clear why the other job is more attractive'

Remember that your original employer may not be that surprised – especially if you are considered top talent.

'Companies – especially big ones – will survive the disappointment,' says Mr Redman. 'You shouldn't be too squeamish about looking after your own prospects.'

How to attract headhunters

It is often assumed that headhunters will find you if and when the time is right – or that if they don't call you, you're not worthy of their attentions. But contrary to popular belief, being headhunted is very much a two-way process.

How do I get noticed?

'You've got to be open to approach,' says Clive Davis, a director of Robert Half, the financial recruitment firm. 'By this I mean put yourself out there and raise your profile. Go to industry events and conferences and become a point of contact and a spokesperson for your company.'

Carole Stone, author of *The Ultimate Guide to Successful Networking*, agrees: 'You need to be the person in the audience who puts their hand up and asks the question or who writes columns for industry newsletters and websites. Get your name known.'

Executive recruitment specialist Moira Benigson says attitude is important, too. 'Be curious and open to new ideas,' she says. 'A lot of people say that they can't do all these things because of their day jobs and become very insular. Then they get to 45 and realize they've never looked outside their companies. That's a very dangerous way to play it these days. You need to nurture your career ... and don't be afraid of taking a calculated risk or jumping. It could be the making of you.'

What about third-party recommendations?

These are greatly valued by headhunters as they come untainted by direct personal interest. 'One of the least talked about but critically important ways of having people recommend you is to be a good boss,' says Mr Davis. 'Headhunters often get valuable information on potential targets by asking more junior staff [that they are placing] who they've worked for and what they are like to work for.'

Ms Benigson says that this works the other way round, too: 'Headhunters often look for people who've worked with star bosses such as Alan Leighton. If you work for people like that you pick up passion and drive and a way of dealing with people. It's like going to INSEAD. If you associate yourself with the best it rubs off – we're always looking for rising stars.'

How subtle must I be?

Although attracting the attention of headhunters usually involves indirect initiatives, Ms Stone says, 'If I was actively looking to move, I'd also very gently drop hints and sow the seeds'.

This more brazen approach is ideally suited to unashamed networking forums, such as professional and alumni associations. 'Alumni networks can be tremendously powerful,' says Mr Davis, 'for both meeting people who might be looking for someone and for suggesting to people that you could be looking for change.'

What should I do when I meet the headhunter?

'Answer questions about your career with specific examples,' says Ms Benigson. 'Tell us where you want to end up and what you want to do. And try to be memorable – tell people something about yourself that makes you stand out.'

Mr Davis says you should cultivate your headhunting contacts like any others. Even if you are not interested in what they are offering at the moment, those in the recruitment industry trade names and recommendations in the same way as other people do.

How to handle references

In these litigious times, references have a reputation for telling people very little that is meaningful. But can you get more out of them – either as a jobseeker or a potential employer?

How important are references?

'Some people don't think they're worth the paper they're written on as candidates tend to give people they got on really well with,' says Nigel Parslow, UK managing director of executive search group Harvey Nash. 'You should treat them with a degree of scepticism – especially personal referees.'

However, they can make the difference in marginal cases and occasionally throw up real surprises. Corinne Mills, joint managing director of Personal Career Management, says that you should think of them as 'the final hurdle candidates have to clear'.

How should I approach references as a candidate?

'You need to manage them,' says Ms Mills. 'Don't put them on your CV unless they are really prestigious and give them only once the offer has been made.'

Make sure you warn referees. 'Call them up and say "This organization will be calling you as a referee. The role is this and they'll be looking for X, Y and Z." Remind them of your achievements. You need to give them the information and make it easy for them.'

What if I have a bad relationship with my boss, or have left under a cloud?

'A lot of people who have this problem give the boss as a referee anyway,' says Ms Mills. 'Don't. Just give someone else instead.'

If you parted acrimoniously, you may need to explain this and offer other people who can vouch for your qualities.

How should I approach references as an employer?

'Don't go down the written route,' says Moira Benigson, founder of executive search firm MBS Group. 'It takes a lot of effort for people to write an e-mail, whereas a phone conversation takes 10 minutes and will tell you far more.'

Ms Mills adds: 'People often won't write stuff down, but they'll give you information off the record. Insist on phone references.'

Listen carefully to what referees say, what they don't say and even their tone of voice. 'Referees will sometimes say something like "You're asking the wrong questions." And if they say hardly anything, that should set alarm bells off too,' says Ms Mills.

Ms Benigson says you should tailor the questions you ask to the role, with a mix of specifics and open-ended questions. 'Ask how good is X at operational delivery. Can they lead from the front? How would people describe them?'

Are there any other sources of reference?

'Recruitment consultants often take soft references – who do you know in that sector who might know of the candidate?' says Mr Parslow.

Social media have a role to play too. 'LinkedIn provides references of a sort, particularly if you get endorsements from people like customers and suppliers,' says Ms Mills.

Writing your CV

With the popularity of business-based social media, the curriculum vitae might seem an anachronism on its way out. But this isn't the case. It remains one of the most basic parts of the job application process and one of the most important. The proliferation of recruitment websites and online business networks means your CV may be widely available already. Potential employers could even be reading it even if you are not looking for a job. Nowadays, your CV isn't something you dust off every five years – it's something you need to update every few months. This, changing ways of working and the availability of professional services mean your CV needs more thought than ever before.

It's just my career history in reverse order, isn't it?

Not any more. CVs have become much more about where you are going and what you have to offer than where you have come from. 'It needs to be a shop window on who you are and show people what you have to offer,' says James Phillips, a senior consultant at The Fuller CV, a CV-writing service.

Elisabeth Marx, a partner at Stonehaven Executive Search, says that, at a senior level, companies are looking for your major achievements: 'We want to see things like successful change management, restructuring, international work, turnrounds and growing the business.'

What are common pitfalls?

You should start by being honest and not exaggerating. The growth of electronic databases means that untruths such as bumped-up academic results are easily uncovered. You should also be very careful about lesser inaccuracies, such as guessing employment dates because you can't remember them, says Sonja Stockton, head of recruitment at PwC – even if these are honest mistakes, they may raise red flags with HR forensics.

Ms Marx says that less is more. 'Sometimes we get 20-page CVs, but, even at a very senior level, they should be no more than two pages – and one page is even better.'

Mr Phillips adds that this minimalist approach should apply to the writing as well. 'CVs are often highly verbose and riddled with clichés. You want to be clear and concise,' he says.

Should I write my own CV?

The argument for doing this is that you know yourself like no one else. But the arguments against are compelling, too. For instance, if you only do something once every five years, you are unlikely to be that good at it and if you spend four days struggling, you may well be better off paying someone else to do it professionally. For those looking to outsource the task, there are companies such as the aforementioned The Fuller CV and The CV House in the UK, and ResumeWriters.com and TheLadders in the USA. Equally, head-hunters and recruiters will often work with you to burnish your résumé. And even if you're writing your own CV, you should seek feedback, preferably from someone who knows the professional you.

Do different countries expect different CVs?

At a senior level, says Ms Marx, there is now a fairly accepted international style. In middle management, however, there are still local idiosyncrasies, 'For instance, a lot of Germans still put their photo on their CV,' she says. And, she adds, Americans, with their focus on presentation and selling, tend to construct stronger CVs.

Anything else?

Avoid silly gimmicks. At one end of the scale, this means that employers don't want fancy fonts and descriptions of your pets under 'outside interests'. And at the other end, it means resisting the urge to make video CVs like Aleksey Vayner's infamous 2006 'Impossible is Nothing', an application to UBS that became a YouTube phenomenon in a way Mr Vayner could never have imagined.

Resignation etiquette

Nobody likes resigning and, as often as not, it's an unpleasant shock for your boss. But you should handle it with tact and diplomacy – and there's far more to it than simply dropping a letter on your line manager's desk.

Why should I worry about resignation etiquette?

'Whenever you quit, you are basically firing your boss and your company,' says Stephen Viscusi, author of *Bulletproof Your Job*. 'When you resign, you're making your line manager look bad so you need to make it clear to them it's not personal.'

It is worth bearing in mind that you may be causing your boss considerable difficulties because these days it is common for those who resign to not be replaced. Even in better economic times, it can take months for a replacement to begin.

'You really need to think through your leaving strategy,' says Nigel Parslow, UK managing director for Harvey Nash Executive Search. 'You should resign with a high degree of humility and empathy.'

Who should I discuss my resignation with?

As well as telling your line manager, you may also have a sponsor or mentor in the company – perhaps the person who brought you in. They should be informed, too.

Once you have resigned, keep it to yourself. Your boss and your company should decide when it is going to become public knowledge. And when you do tell your friends and colleagues, you need to give them the same line you gave your boss.

It leaves a nasty taste if your 'real' reason for leaving gets back to your manager – and it is far more likely to do so when people start to regard you as an ex-colleague.

What if my employer tries to tempt me to stay?

You should always listen to what they have to say because you never know what might have been round the corner. But it is worth remembering that those who accept offers to stay, especially when they are just for more money, often leave fairly soon anyway – and it can be much messier the second time round.

Why should I worry about my old boss when I already have a new job?

An amicable parting of ways will mean that any onerous contractual obligations are unlikely to be enforced. Furthermore, your brilliant new job might not work out – and even if it does, a good relationship with your old boss is something you may wish to fall back on several jobs hence.

'I still get reference calls from people who worked for me seven to nine years ago,' says Mr Viscusi.

While many companies no longer provide formal references, a boss you get on well with may give you an informal reference. Even if external factors such as a takeover mean things have worked out badly for you, you want someone who can explain why you left in a way that reflects well on you. And, of course, if you stay in the same sector, there is always a chance you will run into your boss again.

Surely it is still possible to leave with a bang?

Ten years ago, a churlish exit could be easily airbrushed out of your history. But networking sites, databases and online corporate alumni resources mean your former bosses are far easier to uncover than they once were.

You do not want to be forever haunted by an ill-considered swipe you made in 2009.

Working during your notice period

Once you have decided you are going to leave a job, your relationship with your employer changes fundamentally. How should you make the best of your last days at a company?

How should I behave?

'Whether you've handed in your notice or not, you should carry on working with integrity,' says Moira Benigson, managing partner of MBS Group, an executive search company. 'You never know when you'll need your employers again or when you'll come across them.'

Don't be tempted to download files or pilfer contacts, says Hannah Stratford, head of business psychology at HR consultancy ETS. 'It might seem like a good idea at the time but it isn't. It will make everyone, including your new employer, question your integrity.'

Ms Stratford adds that you also need to stay engaged. 'Having decided you're going to move on, the tendency is to emotionally detach yourself. You should try to resist that. It is very important to continue to be professional. You want to be remembered for the right reasons.'

What if I haven't resigned yet?

This can be very difficult, especially if you know you're leaving long in advance (for instance, if you're moving for family reasons). 'Ideally you'd be honest and open, but you don't want to put your career and salary at risk,' says Ms Stratford.

'It's a high-wire act,' explains John Lees, an executive coach and author of *Take Control of Your Career*. 'How you engage with things like long-term projects can be very tricky. You can't let it slip in passing, but at the same time it is fraudulent to say that you're fully committed to these projects.'

Ms Stratford says: 'You may need to play for time a bit. You might use other work commitments as an excuse not to take on more projects or put another member of your team forward as a developmental opportunity.'

Ms Benigson adds that you need to be careful in the language that you use to describe your current employer: 'Don't bad-mouth your organization to make yourself feel better about leaving or to talk yourself into acting.'

What should I do after I've resigned?

'Offer to help recruit and support your replacement,' says Ms Stratford. 'A smooth transition reflects well on you and a good relationship with your successor means they won't classically blame problems on the last guy.'

Mr Lees takes a similar line: 'Some people work flat out until their last day and don't do any transition. Ensuring knowledge is transferred is more important than finishing every last part of a project.'

He adds that even once you've resigned, you may need to be careful about who you tell: 'People often leak to trusted colleagues and friends before an official announcement is made. But you must give a huge amount of respect to the official channels.'

What if I'm being held to a long notice period?

'Sometimes you might need to plead and beg,' says Ms Benigson. 'I've heard of the CEO of the recruiting company calling up the other CEO to reason with him.'

How to work with the person you will replace

Time spent working alongside the person you're going to replace should be a chance to transfer knowledge and ensure the smoothest of handovers. But not everyone wants to help their successor.

What is the ideal scenario?

Gary Fitzgibbon, a business psychologist, says: 'If someone good is overlapping with you for a few weeks and they're happy to be going and to share what they know with you, then it's a gift.'

John Lees, author of *The Interview Expert* and *How to Get a Job You'll Love*, adds: 'It can be extremely positive and show that a company takes succession planning very seriously.'

How do I avoid problems?

Difficulties typically arise when the incumbent was passed over for the job or there is vagueness about the date of their departure. 'Beware of being a hostage to fortune,' says Mr Lees.

That said, there will be situations where a carrot will be dangled in front of you but without a firm commitment. 'In this situation, the best thing to do is to negotiate a review date as part of the offer,' says Mr Lees. 'It's very easy to be dazzled in the headlights and seduced by the positives. But you have more power to resolve things before you sign on the dotted line.'

How do I deal with someone who resents me?

This usually occurs when your predecessor is an interim who wanted the job themselves.

'It can be difficult,' says executive coach Ros Taylor. 'They might be very bitter, but they might also be the key to the knowledge that you need.' In this case, she explains, 'you need to square up to them and say, "I know you think you should have got the job but I did." Don't pretend they're not there and let the resentment build up.'

Also, be empathetic: tell them they have information you need and use a little flattery to persuade them to help you. Explain that it is better to leave a good legacy rather than a bad one.

Mr Fitzgibbon says: 'It's about building a relationship with them. The animosity will often go after one or two conversations. Don't go in saying how sorry you are that you got the job and they didn't.'

But if the subject comes up, let them have their say. It's like dealing with complaints: you should let people express themselves.'

However, he adds: 'If you can't form a relationship with the person, you should talk to HR... Explaining there are problems now means you're less likely to be blamed later.'

How do I deal with an incumbent who is hanging on?

Typically this happens when you have been given a possibility rather than a firm offer. Ms Taylor suggests: 'You might point out that two people are effectively being paid to do the job and try to get a time limit set on it.'

'If the person is approaching retirement, they may not have come to terms with this.'

However, Mr Fitzgibbon says you need to be realistic about yourself too. 'The possibility of a job is not a job, so treat it with a pinch of salt. It might be hope on your part and a lack of objectivity about your situation.'

Finding a job while working

As the old saying goes, the best time to find a job is when you have a job. But how do you find the hours to do so – and how do you ensure you don't upset your present employer?

How difficult is it?

'It's easier than it was,' says Clive Davis, a director at Robert Half, the financial recruitment firm. 'You can do everything electronically and people are far more flexible. [Recruiters] will also often see you outside normal working hours.' Corinne Mills, managing director, Personal Career Management, says, 'It's always easier to look for a job while you're employed – there are so many networking opportunities with suppliers, customers, conferences and so on. You also have more confidence.'

How should I deal with the need to leave work?

Ms Mills advises against inventing doctor's appointments. 'There's always a danger you can get caught out and that can lead to disciplinary measures. It's better just to say "I have a personal matter to deal with." Or don't say anything. Just explain you need to come in late.'

You have to create time (or take leave) to find a new job. 'People often use lack of time as an excuse,' says Ms Mills. 'If you're doing that, you don't want it enough. Your career is more important than your job.'

Should I tell my employer?

This is not usually a good idea. Justin Spray, a director of business psychologists Mendas, says, 'You can't predict how an employer will react to your looking elsewhere. Some will immediately limit your opportunities or react very emotionally.'

It's natural to feel a bit guilty but you shouldn't get too hung up on this. If you are confronted, the best response is to say that you're committed to the organization, but that it makes sense to be aware of what is on offer.

However, there are times when it's not a bad idea to let your company know that others may be interested in you. 'Having candid conversations with your employer about your career aims should be part of your relationship with your manager,' says Mr Spray. 'A good way of starting [these conversations] might be to tell your boss that you've been approached by a headhunter.'

Can online services help?

Social media are a double-edged sword. This year, a UK executive was sacked for saying on LinkedIn he was interested in career opportunities. 'You need to be very cautious about what you post online,' says Mr Davis. 'Don't over-communicate.' Keep online profiles up-to-date, so the fact that you've recently changed them is no big deal.

However, the web and social media provide fantastic opportunities, even delivering job alerts to your smartphone. Mr Davis adds: 'Because there are so many opportunities out there, you need to be very clear about what you want.'

What should I watch out for?

Ms Mills warns that some unscrupulous companies interview competitors' staff as a means of gathering competitive intelligence. Be very careful what you divulge.

You should also look internally. 'This should be a first resort, not a last resort,' she adds.

Chapter Two
Work and the rest of your life

How to avoid burnout

We are constantly being asked to do more with less, work longer and blur the boundaries of work and life. It's no wonder that work-related stress has become the leading cause of workplace absence. But if you can't avoid stress, how do you mitigate it? How do you prevent yourself becoming overwhelmed by work, and avoid burnout?

What is burnout and what are the signs?

'Burnout is when people get to the end of their personal reserves,' says Kevin Friery, clinical director of Right Corecare, an employee assistance programme provider. 'The well is empty and you're exhausted.' Geraldine Gallacher, executive coach, says: 'If you're not sleeping, are drinking more, beginning to feel angry for no particular reason and losing interest in things that normally excite you, then you're on the road to burnout.' She adds: 'A lot of my clients find themselves in the "tired but wired" phase where they are exhausted but somehow can't rest.'

What are the causes?

'The biggest issue is workload and a long-hours culture,' says Andrea Broughton, principal research fellow at the Institute for

Employment Studies. However, she adds that 'people can manage a big workload if their private life is going well, but when that starts to go wrong, everything else goes wrong'.

Other factors can include reporting to multiple bosses, lack of empowerment, an inability to delegate and someone's underlying mental and physical health.

What steps can I take to prevent burnout?

'Take control of your workload,' says Ms Broughton. 'Ask what you can delegate. Talk through workload issues with your manager and have the confidence to prioritize.' Do not take on more than you can cope with, take breaks and recognize that when it comes to hours worked, less can be more.

Mr Friery says: 'You can develop skills like being calm under pressure. You also need to depersonalize difficult decisions and recognize that they're business choices you're making.' Having good relationships with colleagues reduces aggravation – and you can learn from people who appear to cope well with stress.

What should I do if it all gets too much?

'You need to accept that you can't go on like this, which is easier said than done,' says Ms Gallacher. There is still quite a bit of stigma around talking about stress, but you must. Ideally, speak to someone not involved, such as a coach or a mentor.

'You need people to draw on as your own resources are depleted,' says Mr Friery.

If you do decide to take time off, you must ensure that the organization finds someone to pick up the slack, so you don't come back to the same problem.

What can I do to prevent burnout in those I manage?

'As a manager, you need to set a good example,' says Ms Broughton. 'Don't work weekends. Don't send e-mails at 3am.'

Encourage a culture where people can talk about problems and have the support they need.

For everyone's sake, your own included, have realistic expectations. 'Recognize that they often won't do your bidding perfectly,' adds Mr Friery.

How to work part time

Part-time working is gaining in popularity and is seen by many as a way of finding a balance between career and home life. But how do you go about cutting your hours? And can you really further your career on fewer than five days a week?

Can anyone do it?

Certain roles are better suited to part-time working than others. 'If you're client-facing in any way, it can be really difficult to go part time,' says Miranda Kennett, an executive coach. 'Whereas, if you're in a strategic or planning role, it works far better.'

That said, mobile phones, e-mail and laptops have made part-time work easier for everyone. It is also worth remembering that part-time working may not be doing a certain number of days per week. It could mean doing nine months a year, which works very well for jobs that are project-based.

How do I approach my employer?

'You need to go to your boss with a case,' says Ian Gooden, chief operating officer of HR consultancy Chiumento. 'Don't just say you want to work part time – think about how it can be done and what the benefits are for your employer. It will work if both parties want it to work – and a lot of it comes down to your relationship with your boss.'

He says a good way of pitching it is: 'Would you rather have an excellent person three days or an average person for five?'

With many organizations still looking to cut costs, your employer might well jump at the chance.

What are the practical points to making it work?

'One big thing is flexibility,' says Jennifer Marshall, who works four days a week as an equity partner at Allen & Overy, the law firm. 'I normally work Monday to Thursday, but if I have a meeting I will change it.'

Ms Marshall adds that you need to be in an organization with the right culture, too. 'I get fantastic support at the associate level. We also have a policy that is written down for part-time equity partners. I think that is important – as it means it has the official stamp of approval. Our firm believes in it.'

How do you ensure your job doesn't creep back into your day(s) off?

'You have to be quite firm,' says Ms Kennett. 'But the most difficult thing can often be disciplining yourself. Very conscientious people often do a lot of work at home anyway.'

She suggests that you find something to do on your non-work days. 'Don't fritter the time away, doing things like picking up the dry cleaning.'

Ms Marshall says: 'I tell people I'll be checking my e-mail at such and such a time. That way, they don't expect a response in five minutes.'

She adds that people often ask if she does a five-day job in four days. 'The answer is yes, but previously I was doing a seven-day job in five days, so I don't feel like I'm being short-changed.'

Are there limits?

There is a general consensus that many people can do a full job in four days a week but that once you get to three and below, you start talking about job shares and all that that entails.

Achieving a work–life balance while doing an MBA

Many high fliers struggle with their work–life balance as it is, but what happens when you start doing an executive MBA (EMBA) alongside your job?

What problems am I likely to face?

'It's extremely difficult,' says Cary Cooper, professor of organizational behaviour at Lancaster University Management School. 'You work all day long and then you have to do your [programme] at night. You have to do your course, ensure you show your employer commitment and try and give your family enough time too.'

He notes that the recession has made things even harder. 'Companies have downsized and there's more work for those who remain – and they're more insecure, so they feel the need to be present and they feel guilty when they're out of the office.'

Ilona Simpson graduated from the IESE (Barcelona) global EMBA programme in 2007, during which she was promoted and moved from Germany to the UK. She says: 'There is no balance if you decide to do these things – it's simply a matter of priorities.'

How do you deal with demands from work?

It helps if you can convince your employer that doing an EMBA is not just about your personal career, but is also about the skills that will make you a more productive employee. An understanding manager should let you delegate some of your responsibilities for the duration of your course.

It is also crucial to kiss goodbye to presenteeism. 'You have to identify the things that really matter to your boss and company and concentrate on those,' says Professor Cooper.

'Work hard, but don't work long. In the end, people will judge you by what you achieve.'

Another strategy for managing the juggling act is to seek out projects in your EMBA that overlap with your job – either in terms of subject matter or skill set.

What about demands from outside work?

'Your personal disposable time with your spouse and kids is going to be at a minimum,' says Professor Cooper. 'Unless you have a very supportive spouse, there may be problems at home.'

Ms Simpson notes that EMBAs tend to put stress on any cracks that may exist in a relationship. This means you have to nurture personal and social relationships as they will help support you during your EMBA. Some students have found an ideal solution is for spouses to study for EMBAs together.

Tatiana Quadrello, a senior researcher at The Work Foundation, adds that it is risky to sacrifice your social life: 'We all know how important networks are, both for support and your career. An [EMBA] might take three years to complete. A lot can happen in your life in that time.'

It is important to still take holidays. Indeed, it is worth exploring whether you can extend overseas study terms into family holidays – or even combine them with work trips.

How can I avoid pressure?

Elena Liquete, MBA director at IESE, says it is easier to compart-mentalize if you opt for a modular EMBA with study concentrated into blocks of weeks during the year.

In any case, all EMBAs will have peaks and troughs in work so you should try to plan around these strategically from the outset.

Working fewer hours

We are forever being told to work 'smarter' instead of harder and to find a meaningful work–life balance. But standing in the way of this are a long-hours culture, presenteeism and job insecurity. Is it actually possible to cut down our hours, boost our productivity and go home on time?

What are the arguments for going home on time?

'You need to change your mindset,' says efficiency coach Heather Townsend. 'Unless you actually bill by the hour, it should be about what you put in, not how long you work. Remember, too, that people become unproductive. When you stop being productive, put your hand up. Leave the office and if you have to do an hour later at home, do it.'

Ms Townsend adds that you should find compelling reasons to leave the office, such as meeting friends: 'A lot of people who work long hours do so simply because they have no good reason to leave.'

Do I need to reduce my workload?

Not necessarily – you may just need to plan better. Many people take longer than they should over tasks simply because they approach them chaotically. 'Just take a few minutes out to plan what it is you want to get done,' says Clare Evans, a time management coach.

Fergus O'Connell, author of *Work Less, Achieve More: Great Ideas to Get Your Life Back*, says you need to make realistic commitments too: 'The boss says, "Can you do this by next week?" and you say, "Sure." What you should say is "Let me take a look so I can build a plan." That way you can do it with the least amount of effort and firefighting. A lot of people make unrealistic commitments and, as a result, work very inefficiently.'

You should also build some flexibility into your planning so that minor problems don't throw your whole day out.

Mr O'Connell also recommends ruthless prioritizing. 'People often say "Everything I do is massively important." This isn't true. Figure out what really matters.'

You can also make yourself more productive by taking breaks and restricting time leeches, such as e-mail. 'If you want an instant reply or a discussion, pick up the phone rather than e-mail back and forth,' says Ms Evans.

Can I just say no?

Recognize that your job has boundaries. A lot of people experience a kind of 'role creep', where they constantly take on things they shouldn't be doing. 'Learn to say no nicely,' says Mr O'Connell. 'It's an essential skill. People often think that if they're overworked, they just need to finish the next thing. But if you do that, it never gets any better. Saying no doesn't mean you're not pulling your weight. It means you're saying no to unimportant things.'

What if I work in an office where presenteeism is the norm?

At some point you might have to take a stand. 'There is something to be said for being assertive and standing up for yourself,' says Ms Townsend. 'You may have a boss who works 10- to 12-hour days. But you can set standards upwards as well as downwards. You should also be realistic. How many e-mails and phone calls do you miss by not being there after 6pm?'

If your boss is unhappy with you leaving on time, you may wish to talk about being rewarded on your results. However, Ms Townsend says, the likeliest outcome is: 'You leave on time and nothing happens.'

Working from home

Doing at least part of your job from home has become more popular and much easier during the past decade; indeed, many companies encourage it, not least because they save on office rents. But how do you make the most of it? And when it comes to getting ahead, can out of sight mean out of mind?

Is organizational culture important?

'If you work in a results-based culture and have a lot of support, it might be relatively easy,' says Jane Sullivan, senior consultant at The Work Foundation. 'But if you work for an organization that judges people on how much time they spend in the office then it's much harder. Look at who gets promoted – figure out which one your employer is.'

Roger Delves, director of the MSc in Management at Ashridge Business School, adds: 'It can work better in places where people direct strongly, and less well in more collaborative cultures.'

If your boss is uncertain about letting you do it, you need to agree clear performance targets and prove you can deliver.

Are there any practical points?

'Only do it if you can devote space at home to it,' says Mr Delves. 'Have somewhere separate – so you're going into your professional space. Some people can do this mentally, but most people need to do it physically. It helps avoid mission creep.'

Some people hate working from home. Occasionally this is because they are bad at disciplining themselves, but more often it is simply because they feel isolated. 'Some people energize themselves by being with other people,' says Mr Delves.

Remember that having children around can be problematic, even if a partner is looking after them.

Finally, people often feel privileged but slightly guilty when working at home and, as a result, overwork. 'Of course, no one can see you do this,' notes Ms Sullivan.

How many days you do will vary according to your role. 'Use common sense and be sensitive,' says Ms Sullivan. 'If you're a manager your staff expect to see you and you should want to see them.'

Are some tasks better completed at home?

'I try and do one day a week,' says Monica Burch, chairman of the law firm Addleshaw Goddard. 'It's a bit of space for things you need to really think about – like a speech you have to write. It's very concentrated, productive time.'

Mr Delves adds: 'You spend a lot less time being reactive and responding to other people's needs…It also works very well if you have to deal with people in different time zones.'

How do I manage my visibility?

You may need to blow your own trumpet and make sure those who matter are aware of what you have done, but staying in the loop is just as important. 'In many organizations the important stuff doesn't come through formal networks,' says Ms Sullivan. In fact, if you spend two days a week at home on concentrated productive work, she says, you might want to put more effort into making connections while you are in the office. 'In terms of your career, spending proportionally more time in the office networking might be a better idea.'

You should also be proactive when you're at home. E-mail people, call them, nudge them electronically – this may be enough to create a kind of presence.

Beating stress

Today's work culture means most people are familiar with the symptoms of stress and how to combat it through proper exercise, relaxation and diet. But a deeper understanding of stress is necessary to stop it adversely affecting both your career and your health – and can even help you turn it to your advantage.

Is all stress bad?

Cary Cooper, professor of organizational psychology and health at Lancaster University, says you need to learn to differentiate between stress and pressure, which can be thought of as 'good stress'. 'Pressure is stimulating and motivating and it makes you more productive,' he says. 'A lot of people love pressure… [But] when the pressure becomes greater than your ability to cope then you're in the [bad] stress area.'

What should I look out for?

'Learn to recognize your early warning signs,' says Jessica Colling, product director at corporate well-being consultancy Vielife. These can be behavioural, physical or cognitive – for instance, being irritable, suffering from headaches or a sudden lack of confidence. As many people are poor judges of themselves, she suggests asking a friend or family member to help you spot signs of stress.

What are some of the root causes?

Job insecurities, excessive workloads, bullying bosses, a lack of autonomy or a culture of long hours or micromanagement are all more keenly felt in a downturn. 'There have been so many [job] cuts that workloads have increased massively,' says Professor Cooper. 'People feel guilty about leaving work at a reasonable time and "presenteeism" takes over.'

Ms Colling highlights the role of our own responses to pressure: 'Often we cause ourselves stress through our reactions to situations, rather than the situation itself.'

How do I deal with it?

Recognize that stress becomes a vicious circle and that you need to break the circle by addressing the causes rather than just working harder. Few systems work well when operating flat out, so create time to order your thoughts, plan your tasks and digest what is going on around you. If you are constantly putting in long hours, then create compelling reasons to leave work on time.

'Think of this as a kind of emotional exercise,' says Professor Cooper. 'Even if you enjoy working from eight until eight, in the long term it's not good for you.'

More specifically, if your boss is micromanaging or overloading you, then speak to them. If you manage others, remember that a pressure-cooker environment is likely to impair productivity.

How can I harness 'good' stress?

'Recognize the fact that stress is there and reframe it as a positive thing,' says Octavius Black, founder of the Mind Gym. 'You might think that the best moments in your life are full of stress – they're challenging and difficult. Or you could ask yourself how people you admire would deal with what you consider a stressful situation.'

It is all about managing stress to keep the levels high enough to drive you forward without leaving you overwhelmed. 'Look for the upside and use stress to your advantage,' he says. 'Overcoming difficulties and challenges is how you progress.'

Being fit for the job

Conventional wisdom suggests that being in good physical shape improves most areas of your life, including your career. But how do you strike the right work–Lycra balance – and can you take being fit for the job too far?

How does fitness improve my performance at work?

'It does make a big difference,' says personal trainer Kathryn Freeland. 'There are real mental and physical benefits. You eat better, you feel more energetic, more alert and your head will be clearer. You'll also sleep better, which is really important.'

Doing exercise can also help you cope with stress and it improves the posture of those who are largely desk-bound. Moreover, she says, 'If you're in good shape, you tend to shrug off illnesses better and take less time off sick.'

Octavius Black, founder of the Mind Gym, agrees. 'I remember a teacher saying being fit was worth an extra grade in exams,' he explains. 'You're more likely to be creative and proactive and you'll have more stamina, which is likely to feed into longer-term career success. I'm always impressed with the number of CEOs and senior politicians you see out running in places like Hyde Park.'

How do I fit exercise into my busy schedule?

'If you can [work] it into your commute, you won't have to take time out and you'll be energized when you arrive,' Ms Freeland says. Otherwise, she advises, 'do whatever you'll enjoy and stick with and don't set yourself up to fail by saying you'll go five times a week then getting upset when you only make two. Go on the basis that something will always be better than nothing.'

What should I avoid?

High achievers can be prone to exercise addiction and long workouts every day. But not only do these eat up your time, they are also counterproductive inasmuch as not resting can make you more prone to illness and injury.

Bear in mind that your regime is not that interesting to others, so avoid being an exercise bore. Also remember that sweaty workout clothes are not a badge of honour. 'It's good that people know you bike in, but don't leave your cycling T-shirt on all morning,' says personal branding consultant Jennifer Holloway. 'That sends out the message that you have no self-awareness. If I'm looking for a team leader, I won't choose Mr Sweaty.'

Does it affect how others see me?

'It does change perceptions,' says Ms Holloway. 'If you're out of shape, it's a bit like being scruffy and can lead to the idea that you can't be bothered, whereas if you show people you're willing to invest in yourself, they'll be willing to invest in you.'

People respect those who do something and stick with it – and this is particularly true of weight loss because it's so visible.

'Exercise and sports can be very good for social cohesion and a great way to form a social bond and rapport,' adds Mr Black. 'I cycle and I feel a bond with other cyclists. I know people on boards who have taken up running because the CEO does.'

Chapter Three
Working nicely with others

How to talk people round

Having to implement decisions that employees may not like is a big part of managerial life. So how do you convince your team to follow your lead, especially if it involves a downside for them?

Can I prepare to persuade?

'Plan your influencing strategy carefully,' says Melanie Long, a business psychologist at talent measurement specialists SHL. 'People change at different times. You should focus on those who have influence in the group. Identify role models and use the political mechanics of the organization to target stakeholders.'

Your position will also be greatly strengthened if you develop a good rapport with people by helping them, says Steve Martin, co-author of *Yes! 50 Secrets from the Science of Persuasion*. 'You are at your most influential immediately after someone has said "thank you" so build up obligations beforehand.'

How do I present the decision?

You need to appeal to hearts and minds. 'Leaders often come up with really strong rational arguments,' says Ms Long. 'But they don't include people so they feel part of it. Tell a story, appeal to people's emotions, and put yourself in their shoes. Consult widely and act on this input, rather than presenting it as a fait accompli.'

Jessica Pryce-Jones, CEO of performance consultancy iOpener, says that fear of the unknown needs to be dispelled. 'Connect back to times where similar actions have worked,' she says.

You should also recognize that influence is an ongoing process. 'The process is like presenting a two-year-old with a Brussels sprout,' says Ms Pryce-Jones. 'You don't change it, but you do try to make it palatable.'

What about me?

'Lead by example,' says Ms Pryce-Jones. 'You have to share the pain as well.'

One of the reasons that, historically, Japanese CEOs have had relatively little difficulty persuading staff to take pay cuts is because they so often take brutal ones themselves.

Mr Martin says that you should not tell people: 'You should do this because of my position in the hierarchy or because it comes from the top.' It is better to be seen as someone who is in a position of authority.

If you are speaking to an audience you don't know well, he says, one of the best things you can do is tell them why they should listen: 'credentialize yourself'. You can mention externalities, such as the economy, but to dwell on them too much can look like you are trying to avoid responsibility.

What about those I can't talk round?

'Do mention payback,' says Ms Pryce-Jones. 'Say, "I don't like having to do this, but when things get better you'll be the first people whose efforts are recognized."'

But along with the carrot, you should also invoke the stick. Make it clear that if they don't take the action, there will be negative effects on other team members and third parties and their relationships with them.

Mr Martin says: 'You can also appeal to [personal] loss. It sounds counter-intuitive but people are very risk averse. Say this is what you could lose if you don't take action.'

Being a good team player

Advice on how to be a leader, a maverick and a standout is everywhere. But nowadays nearly all of us work collaboratively in teams and being able to play nicely with others is hugely important. So how do you strike the right balance between your own ambition and being a team player?

Why is being a team player so important?

'Almost everyone is part of a team in some sense,' says Graham Abbey, an executive coach at March Friday. 'The ability to work together is incredibly important. If everyone was challenging the status quo and pushing boundaries all the time, you'd have chaos.'

What are the keys to working in a team?

'You need the capacity to understand other people and to see things from their perspective,' says Robert Myatt, a director at business psychologists Kaisen. 'Look for the sources of reciprocity and collaboration. What are the currencies – such as time and expertise – that you can trade?'

Ian Gooden, chief operating officer of HR consultancy Chiumento, says: 'Recognize and value diversity in working styles – you don't want a whole team of big-picture thinkers.' You should also look at motivation: 'Not everyone is there for the same reasons you are. Understand what makes people tick.'

How do I deal with disagreements?

'A lot of it is about self-awareness,' says Mr Abbey. 'Where can you make compromises that aren't that important to you but mean a lot to others? You need to achieve your goals without stepping on too many toes and know which battles to fight.'

However, there can be too much harmony. 'You see plenty of situations where a desire not to rock the boat means that you don't see big risks,' says Mr Abbey. 'If everyone plays too much for the team, you can get a kind of groupthink and an abdication of personal responsibility.'

What about recognition?

'You need to put yourself somewhere between being too self-aggrandizing and hiding your light under a bushel,' says Mr Myatt. 'Make sure the right people know the right things about you. Don't believe that your achievements will speak for themselves but don't build your reputation at the expense of others.'

Are senior teams different?

'As you get higher up, the nature of teams changes,' says Mr Abbey. 'Many people see teams as rallying behind one unifying cause. But, at a senior level, people may have very different goals. So being a good team player at this level requires recognizing many different agendas and can be very political. It is about managing short-term objectives and longer-term relationships.'

How do I deal with difficult colleagues?

'Ultimately, this is the responsibility of the leader,' says Mr Myatt. 'If the leader is unaware of this, talk to them but show them the evidence rather than offering opinion.'

As singling out individuals can be difficult and demoralizing, Mr Myatt suggests building a contract with each other. 'Agree how things will be done and you'll have a document to go back to.'

That said, if you can speak frankly to each other, you should. 'One of the great themes in high-performing teams is the ability to give each other feedback,' says Mr Gooden.

Working with people you don't like

Colleagues are like family – you don't get to choose them. So how do you create a decent working relationship with those you don't like?

How do I approach the situation?

'We tend to think that we should get on very well with everyone in the office,' says Graham Abbey, an executive coach at March Friday. 'But it's not like that – and like and dislike are very different to active dislike. It can be enough to focus on the work, not the person. You also need to ask yourself how significant they are. If you can avoid them easily, they're not significant.'

Alan Redman, a business psychologist with the Criterion Partnership, says: 'There are plenty of people who are mildly irritating. It becomes a real issue when you find the person teeth-grindingly awful and you have to spend a lot of time with them.'

Whatever the case, you should address these problems rather than let them fester and grow.

Can I make it better?

'Dig into why you dislike them,' says Mr Abbey. 'When we find something we dislike about people, we tend to focus on that and dwell on it.' It helps if you separate the behaviours from the person too. So, instead of disliking Bob, it might be that you just dislike the way Bob talks loudly on the phone or eats egg sandwiches.

Mr Redman says that you need to change the dynamic. 'You want to move on from antagonism to acceptance,' he explains. 'You accept that they're irritating and deal with it. You might even get to alteration, where you're in a position where you can work on both the other person and yourself.'

Ask what the situation says about you, adds Mr Abbey. 'Am I being less tolerant than I could be?'

Can I confront them?

Again, you need to make it about the behaviour, not the individual, because nobody likes being told that you hate them.

'Use classical feedback techniques,' says Mr Abbey. 'Tell them about the effect their behaviour has on you. Sometimes they won't even be aware that they're doing it.'

Mike Leibling, author of *Working With the Enemy*, suggests a diplomatic approach. 'Confront the issue without being confrontational. You might say to them: "You and I haven't got on brilliantly in the past. What do I need to do?"'

What are the coping strategies?

Talking to others may help you see this person in a different light, Mr Abbey says.

Mr Leibling adds: 'You need to remember that it's perfectly normal not to get on with a certain percentage of people… Have a sense of humour and turn it into a joke. Try not to carry the person around in your head, but if you do, cut them down to size. Don't let them become a monster.'

What if I've tried everything and I still can't bear them?

Your first option here is to talk to your boss. If this fails you may have to move – either departments or even companies.

Mr Leibling cautions that you should not view this as a nuclear option. 'It's important to remember that getting out is not the last resort,' he says. 'It's the next-to-last resort: the last resort is a heart attack or a breakdown – and getting out can be a very good decision. If you're at a party you don't like, it's not the party for you.'

How to ask for help

Many people would often rather suffer in silence for months than ask a colleague or a superior for help. They think it reflects badly on them and that only incompetents need assistance. This is far from the truth. We should worry less and ask more.

Is there anything wrong about asking for help?

'Leaders and managers tend to assume others will ask for help as and when they need it, but they hugely overestimate how likely people are to do so,' says Francis Flynn, professor of organizational behaviour at the Stanford Graduate School of Business. 'What prevents people from asking for help is a great fear of appearing incompetent and a desire not to impose.' Both fears, he adds, are unfounded. 'What you tend to forget is that people get something very positive out of helping others and organizations actually want this kind of cooperation.'

Corinne Mills, managing director of Personal Career Management, agrees: 'Not asking for help and letting problems build up are actually a weakness and can make you a liability.'

Do I need to prepare to ask?

'There's nothing worse than ignoring someone for ages and then suddenly asking for their help,' says corporate psychologist Ben Williams. 'You want to set up a network of people you know well so that when the time comes you can go to them for help – and if you help other people, they will want to help you.'

Ms Mills says: 'You should ask for help in a timely manner. Ask when you think you might have a problem, not when everything's already gone horribly wrong. You don't want people saying "Why didn't you ask sooner?"'

Who should I ask?

It depends on the problem. Possibilities include your manager or other colleagues you know well.

For serious problems, the trick is often to contact people who are informed but not overly involved. Many companies have employee assistance schemes with advice lines, while others provide mentors.

Is there a right way to ask?

Good manners and a little charm never go amiss. 'Say, "You obviously have a lot of experience in this area and I'd be very grateful if…"' suggests Mr Williams. 'It's not so much flattery as acknowledging why you're approaching the person.'

Be very specific about what you want and try to anticipate problems. If you are asking for help with a process you do not understand, says Mr Williams, 'describe your goals to the person in question. Be very clear what you want to achieve.'

If it is a personal matter, provide as much information as you can. 'Everyone has an inner life and employers do have a duty of care to employees,' says Ms Mills.

What if they say no or ignore the request?

'In some organizations you do have to scream before you get help,' says Ms Mills. 'If you've been rebuffed and there are serious implications, it's worth putting it in writing in an e-mail to ensure that you're covered.'

However, this is a last resort and in the first instance you should always do it in person. 'Unless it's trivial, never ask for help via e-mail. It's much more difficult to refuse a request for help when it's done face to face,' says Mr Williams.

How to apologize

Saying sorry at work is often difficult, especially as many see it as a tacit admission of weakness. It shouldn't be. Rather, your goal should be to offer a good apology that leaves you stronger and enhances your reputation. To achieve this means striking a balance between contrition and not undermining your own position.

Why do people struggle with apologies?

'Some people believe saying sorry is a sign of weakness and an admission of wrongdoing that can damage your prospects,' says corporate psychologist Ben Williams.

'But the reverse is true. It's a sign of tremendous strength and confidence. Mistakes are also learning experiences, and it is important to acknowledge them.' Virginia Merritt of Stanton Marris, the strategic leadership consultancy, adds: 'Apologizing for wrong judgment calls is becoming a powerful demonstration of real leadership. It can be a very brave thing to do and can really humanize leaders.'

What makes a good apology?

'The important thing is that you have to mean it,' says etiquette consultant William Hanson. 'If you don't, there's no point in apologizing.'

Mr Williams says there is a certain structure to a good apology. 'If you need to give an explanation, do it beforehand so it doesn't sound like justification. Use "I" language not "you" language: "I'm sorry I was late" rather than "It can be difficult to get to your meetings on time."

'Anticipate negative reactions by using phrases like "I know you're upset. I didn't mean anything by it." Listen and use listening body language.'

For big public apologies, Ms Merrit says a narrative is a good idea. 'I saw one leader talk about his moment of truth and tell people when he recognized what he had done wrong,' she says. 'It had a huge impact on the people in the room.'

She adds that an apology needs to be backed up by action. 'If it's behavioural, rather than judgemental, you need to make a commitment to change and ask for feedback. It can't be just a mea culpa.'

If you are unsure about what you are doing, it is worth practising on a friend or a trusted colleague beforehand. But make sure you explain the situation neutrally: if you show yourself in an overly flattering light, their comments will not be worth much.

What should I avoid?

'You need to ensure that any explanation doesn't become an excuse, as this will make the other person feel like you haven't bought into the message,' says Mr Williams.

Ms Merritt warns that if you are a leader it can be difficult – and even feel wrong – to apologize for collective decisions. 'But you should. That is what is expected of leaders and hiding behind the team makes you look like you are dodging responsibility,' she says.

What if my colleagues are just being oversensitive?

Mr Hanson advises that, although it may rankle, an apology is often the easiest course of action. 'They may be overly sensitive but, in terms of your productivity and working life, it's better to be on good terms with everyone.'

What if my apology is not accepted?

'If they really won't accept that you've apologized, there is not a lot you can do but at least you know you've done it,' says Mr Hanson.

How to take praise

How to give positive feedback is a frequently discussed management dilemma, but being the recipient of praise can be equally difficult.

How should I react to praise?

'The first thing is to acknowledge the praise and say thank you,' says business psychologist Ben Williams. 'Some people are happy to do this, while others find it awkward. But even if you're the shy type, you should make the effort.'

Adrian Moorhouse of the organizational development consultancy Lane4 says that the emotionally intelligent response is to engage, using positive body language: 'Look the person in the eye. If you look away or at your feet, you might think you're being humble but you can appear ungracious. Front up and be interested. It's like getting a nice gift – you pay attention to it.'

Etiquette expert William Hanson adds: 'A lot of people's knee-jerk reaction is to compliment back and this can sound insincere. Don't do it. Instead, make a mental note and if you return the compliment, do so at a later date.'

Is receiving praise important?

Mr Moorhouse explains it is crucial in encouraging the confidence of employees. 'It's quite fundamental,' he says.

It is also an opportunity to start a discussion. 'Ask where specifically you did well. Is there something you can do that builds on this?'

What if I work in a low-praise environment?

'If people aren't praising you, you're probably doing fine,' says Mr Hanson. 'You rarely write a letter of thanks to a hotel you enjoyed staying in. It's often not in our nature to compliment.'

Mr Williams notes that in some sectors, if everything is working as it should be, that is seen as evidence of a job done well. But he adds that you can help create a culture of praise: 'If you want praise from your boss, praise them. Don't be smarmy but acknowledge them and the work they do.'

Can I use the praise afterwards?

Repeating it can sound boastful. 'Don't talk publicly about praise given in private,' says Mr Williams. However, he adds, it is good form to tell others if the compliments affect them. 'If someone praises you for a job, do pass it on to others involved in the project.'

It is worth jotting down the details of verbal good feedback as it can be useful in your next appraisal.

What if you think it's a backhanded compliment?

If in doubt, take it well: many managers are bad at giving feedback and they may simply be being clumsy. 'There are generation gaps and gender gaps,' says Mr Williams.

Mr Hanson says: 'If it is meant badly, the best thing is not to rise to it. If it's part of a pattern you could fight back or say: "I know you think you're being funny but… "' However, he adds: 'In many offices backhanded compliments are a form of humour. Respond in kind.'

How to be a boss, not a friend

Managers should aim to create a pleasant and convivial working environment. But how do you ensure you don't fall into the trap of becoming your employees' friend rather than their boss?

How do I treat employees?

Being liked and being respected aren't an either/or proposition. 'The problem is we tend to select managers on technical competencies, not personal and social competencies,' says Cary Cooper, professor of organizational psychology at Lancaster University Management School. 'If we did, we'd see less stress and higher morale and productivity.'

Professor Cooper says you should listen to people when they talk about their personal lives and not be afraid to open up a bit yourself. 'There's a psychological contract,' he explains. 'It says: "I'll be human and humane, but you have to deliver." The loyalty you get is great.'

Antoinette Oglethorpe, a leadership development consultant at Workmaze, says: 'The single biggest thing you can do as a boss is show appreciation; people often just don't give positive feedback. Don't do it in a "Cheers, good job" way; rather, say: "You made a difference and this is why."'

You should also aim to give staff a real sense of ownership. Seek their views on decisions and explain the context of what is being done. But give them some genuine skin in the game too, whether it's via low-priced options or a profit-share scheme.

How about factors beyond the interpersonal?

Free fruit and coffee will make the office a better place. But there are other little things you can do too. 'For high performers be flexible about timekeeping,' says Hannah Stratford, head of business psychology at human resources consultants ETS. 'If someone needs to leave at 4.30 to play football, let them go, but equally you need to say no when people aren't performing.'

What if I find myself crossing the line between boss and friend?

'It is very easy to become friends with those you manage,' says Ms Stratford, adding that the modern workplace, with its emphasis on informal networks and relationships as ways of getting things done, practically encourages this.

In some ways, however, the atmosphere you want to create is more like that of a happy family with a head than a social group of peers. 'You want to make decisions that your staff will thank you for in the long term, not the short term,' says Ms Oglethorpe.

How do I deal with unpleasant decisions?

'Sometimes a manager just has to be comfortable in uncomfortable situations,' says Ms Stratford. 'You might have to withhold information or make collective decisions with your peers that are best for the company but not best for members of your team.' She adds: 'I do think you can bring in a personal element even in formal processes like redundancy.'

Professor Cooper says that in these cases you often reap the rewards of having built good relationships earlier on: 'When you have to give staff bad news, they're more likely to take it well if they know you care.'

Working for two bosses

The difficulties of working for more than one person have been recognized since Biblical times (Matthew 6:24, 'No man can serve two masters'). The trouble is, with project-based work and matrix structures, having several bosses is becoming ever more prevalent.

What difficulties am I likely to encounter?

'You might have conflicting priorities, two people saying their tasks are urgent and you may even encounter jealousy,' sums up executive coach Miranda Kennett.

John Gibbs, people partner for corporate finance at PwC, says problems arise when you overcommit. 'Often this happens when several projects go into a final phase together.'

What can I do to prevent problems?

The keys things to strive for are organization and clarity. 'Set out what you're trying to achieve,' says Jane Clarke of business psychologists Nicholson McBride. 'Get it signed off and agreed and then have it reviewed often. You might want to have a regular three-way call. This can be very helpful as it allows you to prioritize competing agendas.'

If the two bosses cannot agree on priorities, 'Ask what the business requires. Refer to common purposes.'

Ms Kennett says you need honesty about urgency: 'You should establish what the real timetables are.'

She says that it is human to try to please everyone and overreach yourself but that you need to avoid that temptation. 'Make sure you have a job description. When you're coping well, people tend to pile things on you, but you need to watch this. Often tasks are delegated just because your manager doesn't like doing them.'

Above all, Mr Gibbs advises: 'Have these conversations early. Problems will be sorted and your reputation enhanced.'

What general workplace skills can help me?

'Build strong relationships,' says Mr Gibbs. 'These and a good history of delivering will give you some wiggle room if there are problems. It's also important to flex your style to suit the two different managers.'

Ms Clarke says, 'You need to master the art of handling conflict, saying no and having difficult conversations.'

What if things get on top of me?

'Its better to be honest and come clean rather than struggle and eventually let everyone down,' says Mr Gibbs.

If the problem is the two bosses being unable to agree your priorities, Ms Kennett says, 'Try and get them in a room together to talk. You may even need a third person to facilitate.'

Are there any upsides?

'You'll get known more widely and the flexibility you gain working for people with different styles is a good thing,' says Mr Gibbs.

Ms Clarke adds: 'At least you haven't got all your eggs in one market. If you only have one boss and they get canned, you could be in trouble.'

A boss you don't respect

Working for a manager you do not respect can be difficult. But if you examine why you don't respect them you may find things are not as bad as they seem. And even if you discover that you cannot respect your boss, there may be other ways of motivating yourself.

How important is it?

'The single biggest determinant of engagement is your relationship with your boss,' says David Pendleton, a founder of Edgecumbe, the organizational psychologists. 'It affects everything from how long you stay to your discretionary effort. People join a brand but they leave a manager.'

Blaire Palmer, managing director of Taming Tigers, a coaching consultancy, says: 'Whether they'll admit it or not, the number-one thing most people want to do in their job is to please their manager, so it is a very significant issue if you don't respect them.'

Is the problem you?

'It may be perception, not reality,' says Ms Palmer. 'You might admire a firm hand but your manager may be a collaborator and a listener, so you think they're wet and a drip. The job of leading people is an art, not a science, and you may not understand their methodology.'

John Hoover, author of *How to Work for an Idiot*, says: 'We're socialized to rebel against authority and often wind up taking out unresolved adolescent issues on those above us for the rest of our lives. You should question your own motives. Beware of your inner idiot.'

It is also worth asking yourself whether the problem is dislike rather than disrespect. If this is the case, it may be enough to realize that you will never be friends, but recognize that the boss is effective and gets the job done.

How can I resolve issues of respect?

Mr Pendleton says you should ask why the person acts as they do. For instance, you might think your boss leaves early because they are lazy and then discover it's because they have a very ill child. 'A lot of problems come down to misattribution errors,' he says.

Can I work for a boss if respect is impossible?

Your boss is very important but they are not the only reason to be positive about what you do. 'Find other sources of engagement,' says Ms Palmer. 'It might be the work itself, it could be career development or it might be colleagues you like and respect.'

She adds that you may be able to find substitute bosses too: 'You could build a good relationship with your boss's boss or find a mentor.'

Mr Hoover adds that working for a poor boss also has upsides. 'If the boss is an idiot, you can respect yourself for developing the skills to work round that person.'

He adds that even if no one on your team respects the boss, there are better ways of dealing with this.

'Rather than fall into groupthink where everyone badmouths the boss, be the person who shows everyone else how you can deal with them,' he says. 'Remember that nobody advances their career by making their boss look stupid – and if they really are stupid, they'll do it themselves.'

Chapter Four
Networks, power and influence

How to network

The ability to leverage your business connections has become more important as we have moved from jobs for life to portfolio careers. For most people, it is now right up there with hard work, management skills and ambition in terms of bringing opportunities your way. While old-style school and university networks still exist, factors from flatter hierarchies to social media mean that networking has never been more democratic, accessible or important.

How and where do I do it?

Chances are you network to some extent already. Nonetheless, every event you attend is a potential opportunity. If you want a few points of entry, places such as local business groups and entrepreneurs' associations are worth looking at and there are dedicated networking organizations such as BNI.

Failing these, you could set up your own group. 'Hold a regular get-together of colleagues on the same day, at the same time and at the same venue for, say, four weeks running,' says Carole Stone, author of *The Ultimate Guide to Successful Networking*. 'Keep it to one-and-a-half hours maximum, otherwise people miss each other.'

Unless you're a natural, meeting people at events is a bit of an art form

Decide who you want to target and do some research on them – most people respond well to interest. As with most introductions, a mutual acquaintance is best, but failing that, you can just introduce yourself – and if you have done your homework you should be able to find some kind of shared interest. You need to bring something to the party, too – it is not enough to show up and expect a business card. You don't actually need to spend that long with people unless you're getting on like a house on fire – a few minutes will do. But when you do leave them you should try to introduce them to someone else before doing so.

Take a practical approach to who you speak to

A Fortune 500 chief executive may be about as interested in networking with you as you are in networking with your neighbour's pet, so someone a couple of ranks down may be a better target.

It is unwise to brush off junior people as unimportant. 'Remember, the PA is the gatekeeper to your meeting the top person and should be kept in the loop and treated well,' cautions Ms Stone.

Besides, today's junior executive could be tomorrow's senior executive and favours done to those at the beginning of their careers can be an excellent long-term investment.

Perhaps the best way to think about networking is that it's a bit like business karma: good deeds are likely to be rewarded.

What about electronic networking such as LinkedIn and Facebook?

These have changed the world of networking in a number of ways: they have made it far easier; they are a fantastic way of keeping tabs on those you network with; and, in a world where increasing numbers of people have working relationships with large numbers of people they have never met, they can act as a kind of virtual networking organization.

That said, it is worth remembering that a lot of these connections are made because people are too polite to say no. Moreover, something that requires so much less effort is unlikely to result in the kind of personal connection that a real meeting does. Best, then, to use social networks as a kind of adjunct to face-to-face networking.

How to work the Christmas party

The company Christmas party can be a surprisingly useful opportunity to enhance your career prospects and make valuable contacts. But it is important to get the balance between work and play right.

How do I approach the party?

'Remember that the Christmas party is not work,' says David Pendleton, a founder of Edgecumbe, the organizational psychologists. 'It's a completely different way to interact with people who you may normally only discuss tasks with, but it's still a work event.'

Networking expert Carole Stone says it is an opportunity to build on existing relationships and to talk to colleagues that you do not normally deal with. 'It's an opportunity to look sideways outside your area. You never know who you'll meet and what you'll learn,' she says.

How do I work the party?

'The biggest area is connections and networks,' says Simon Hayward, managing partner of Cirrus, the employee engagement specialist. 'It's also an opportunity to use a bit of disclosure and to find out a bit about people and to build a bit more trust. Trust is a huge enabler.'

But Mr Hayward says there is no point faking an interaction. 'Don't be manipulative, be genuine and have fun together. It allows barriers to come down so you can know people on a more intimate level,' he says. 'When you make those intimate connections, it means you can offer favours and pull in favours. It removes formality and can be much better than a business meeting. There's value to the individual and the organization.'

What about talking to senior people?

'If there's someone you want to meet, this is the perfect opportunity,' says Mr Hayward. 'The layers of the organization are much vaguer. But remember it's a party – make conversation interesting and genuine, don't just pursue an agenda and don't forget the marketing director is human.'

Ms Stone says being tactful is important. 'If you are sitting next to the CEO, don't say: "I have this idea." Rather, talk to them, then at the end ask if you can send them an e-mail or drop in to see them,' she says.

How formal should I be?

'Don't be a party pooper,' says Ms Stone. 'Talk to everyone – and if you drink, have a couple of drinks.'

Mr Pendleton warns, however, that the situation will dictate the level of formality – so be careful about alcohol. 'You can be a bit bolder, but be personally sensitive like you would at any social function,' she says. 'Avoid the mistletoe and don't drink too much – in whole-company events, serious errors of judgement get around like wildfire.'

How should I follow up with people I've met?

'Drop them an e-mail afterwards,' says Mr Pendleton. 'Remember: relationships are fed by regular contact. Send them a link that might be of interest or follow them on Twitter. It takes 15 seconds. Technology has made following up so much easier.'

Handling important people

Meeting very senior people can be a big opportunity but it is also a potential minefield – and has much in common with meeting celebrities or sporting heroes. So how do you ensure you make the most of your time with them and a leave a good impression?

How do I prepare?

'You need to understand who you're dealing with,' says Dirk Schlimm, author of *Influencing Powerful People*. 'Talk to people who've met them.'

Peter Godfrey, an entrepreneur and corporate adviser, says: 'Practise a speech that's a few minutes long. Have a start, a middle and an end. Think about a few good points you want to get across.'

How should I behave?

Popular culture would have us believe that CEOs love upstarts who speak truth to power. But this is rarely true. 'There's often very little upside – and considerable downside – to telling a senior person the unvarnished truth about themselves,' says Rob Yeung, a psychologist at Talentspace and author of *I is for Influence*. 'The messenger can get shot.'

Instead, you want to adapt to how they do things and behave with diplomacy. 'Let them know you understand who you're dealing with,' says Mr Schlimm. 'Show them you get it.'

Mr Godfrey says it's a mistake to assume that a senior person will know more than you do as they tend to have an overview. In fact, if you're being asked to a meeting for your knowledge, this can make things quite easy.

Far trickier, says Mr Schlimm, is when you're asked for an opinion. 'Try and say things like, "Is this too risky?" rather than "This is too risky." Be non-confrontational and indirect. You don't want to be put in your place.'

For these reasons, first-hand stories that illustrate points are very good.

What about social situations?

Many of the same rules apply. 'If you're making small talk, larger-than-life executives often have a wide range of interests and probably love to hear about your hobbies,' says Mr Schlimm. 'But even here, make sure you're talking about something you know well.'

Mr Yeung suggests: 'Treat them as you would someone older at a wedding that you're meeting for the first time. You don't know their rules and need to conduct yourself in a certain way.'

If you're stuck for something to say, ask open-ended, general questions and listen; it is better to be remembered as a good listener than someone who said too little – or too much.

What if things go wrong?

People often make gaffes when an important person lets their guard down, so you need to keep reminding yourself that they're not an old friend.

If things do go bad, says Mr Schlimm, 'shut up and listen. If they start getting upset with you, don't put more fuel on the fire. Don't try and talk your way out. Instead, project back to them.'

If they remain offended, Mr Yeung suggests, 'you should demonstrate great contrition. Most people will accept an apology.'

Mr Schlimm adds that you need to watch out for yourself too: 'Powerful, charismatic people can sometimes take you places you don't want to go. Decide where your line is and consider finding an accountability partner.'

How to work a room

How many of us have faced a room full of people, wishing we could be one of those confident types who glides effortlessly from group to group? But chances are, it does not come naturally to them either. So how can you become one of those people?

Can I prepare?

'It's a good idea to get a guest list beforehand and pick out the people you want to meet,' says Carole Stone, author of *The Ultimate Guide to Successful Networking*.

Miranda Kennett, founder of First Class Coach, says: 'You need to get over your antipathy and put yourself in the role of a detective. Tell yourself that there are interesting and useful people in that room and your role is to find them.' Even if you do not know who is in the room, it is a good idea to go in armed with a couple of generic icebreakers.

What if I really struggle with these events?

'The alternative,' says Ms Stone, 'is not to work the room, which is really stupid, given that you're already there. If it helps, say to yourself, "I'll stay for 40 minutes and talk to three people."'

Jane Clarke, a director at business psychologists Nicholson McBride, says that many people worry that they will have nothing to say or feel morally wrong about schmoozing. The trick is to reframe these thoughts. 'Paradoxically, people who are somewhat introverted are actually better at meeting people once they overcome their reluctance because they listen as well as talk and they're not as boorish as extroverts,' she explains.

How do I meet people?

Anyone standing alone probably feels as you do, so go and introduce yourself. If you cannot find anyone by themselves in the room, you will probably find them at the bar. Failing that, work your way into a group. 'Just be honest,' says Ms Stone. 'Say you don't know anyone there.'

And go in with the right mindset: that you will bring something interesting to the conversation.

How do I get away from people?

If you only want five minutes with people, they probably only want five minutes with you. 'It's always best to leave people wishing you'd said a little more,' advises Ms Stone.

The best way to leave someone is by introducing them to someone else before moving on, rather like an occupational dance. You should never sit down as that makes it much harder to move on. And, for those with a more devious streak, there are plenty of tricks. Ms Stone says: 'I used to know a man who always carried two glasses of wine, so he could always say, "If you'll excuse me, I have to deliver this."'

What should I avoid?

Obviously you should not get too drunk or spit canapés on to your new acquaintance. Ms Kennett warns you should not go in for the kill either. 'It's a real mistake to make a big sales pitch to someone you've just met. All you should aim to do is break the ice and exchange details,' she says.

Ms Clarke adds you should also try to find a good level with whomever you are talking to: 'Don't come across as overly confident if you're speaking to someone your junior or overly subservient if you're speaking to someone above you.'

Building a power base

People often associate building power with being terribly underhand. But in reality it simply involves managing things like trust, loyalty and influence rather than anything more Machiavellian.

Why do I need a power base?

'In the modern workplace your responsibility exceeds your formal power,' explains Jo Owen, social entrepreneur and author of *Power at Work: The Art of Making Things Happen*. 'We no longer command

and control. In order to get things done, you need to have a broad alliance of people you can influence and whose support you can count on. Having a power base is about making things happen. People talk about your IQ and your EQ but they often forget your PQ – your power/political quotient. You really need all three to get ahead.'

What are the basics?

'There are three factors at work,' says Ceri Roderick, a partner at occupational psychologists Pearn Kandola. 'There's what you know: key information that makes you a go-to person. There's what you're good at: things you can do that others can't. And there's who you know and the relationships you build.'

It is not so much about being liked, but more about being trusted and being seen as someone who can deliver. Peter Shaw, an executive coach at Praesta, says that being powerful is 'being regarded as someone whose views are sought out'.

How do I go about it?

Build your base incrementally, one person and one event at a time. 'An important aspect is having followers,' says Mr Shaw. 'Show interest in people's development and introduce them to opportunities.'

Of course, you will need to be tough with people sometimes, but dealing with difficult problems head on will improve your standing in the long run.

Mr Owen says that for a truly effective power base, you need to have the right role in the right company. Large multinationals often have places where CEOs tend to be groomed – be it geographic (such as a French company's Paris HQ) or functional (such as the marketing department at Procter & Gamble).

'People often imagine power is about grabbing positions and holding money,' says Mr Shaw. 'But it's usually much more subtle. I once knew someone who built up a big power base by judging which were the right meetings to attend – where the key players were. He went to them and made sure he asked the right questions.'

What does not work?

Mr Roderick says that being sycophantic is something senior managers will recognize. 'You need to bring something to the relationship.'

He also says that in spite of the stereotypes, steer clear of under-handedness. 'Most people are very keenly attuned trust detectors and very, very good at spotting when you're faking it.'

What about moving to another organization?

When you move organizations you often start again from square one. 'If you've been somewhere 10 years, you build up a very elaborate network of influence and trust,' says Mr Owen. For this reason, you should try to extend your network of influence beyond your own business – for instance, through suppliers and customers.

Chapter Five
Keeping up
appearances

How to rebrand yourself

Whether you're worried that colleagues see you as a little steady and dull or you're moving into a new position and concerned about the impression you're going to make, the idea of treating yourself as a brand that needs refreshing from time to time is one that's gaining increasing currency in the workplace.

Is rebranding just like a makeover?

Far from it. Like businesses, individuals often need to rebrand themselves when perceptions do not accurately reflect the underlying reality. 'You might have joined a business very young and grown up,' says Wally Olins, chairman of Saffron Brand Consultants, 'but people still perceive you as the office junior.'

Equally, it could be that part of who you are is having a disproportionately negative impact on your overall image – for example, a messy desk could cast you as disorganized, or a tendency to raise your voice could lead to the perception that you are unreasonable.

Are there any easy wins?

There are plenty of little, cosmetic things that can tarnish your brand, says Kim Fletcher, managing director of Trinity Management Communications. 'I used to cycle in and instead of changing immediately, I'd answer a call and before I knew it, I'd been working for an hour in scruffy old clothes,' he says. 'Looking like that at your desk does belittle you in other people's eyes.'

Addressing areas such as this is a quick way to brush up your workplace image. 'Try and see yourself through your colleagues' eyes and write down a list of things you need to work on,' he says.

What if my brand has more fundamental problems?

In this case, you may need to dig deeper. 'The key is discovering what people find compelling about you and building on that foundation,' says Louise Mowbray, a personal branding consultant. She suggests you go to your 'market' or 'audience' – colleagues, senior managers or suppliers – and ask them how they perceive you, what irritates them and what they like. Then work on the bad points and deliver on the good ones. 'It's about adding value and giving people what they want consistently,' she says. 'Consistency builds trust in a personal brand.'

You need to find your niche, then get your name out as the person to go to for whatever it is. Ms Mowbray adds that this should be subtle: 'Arrange for a speaker to come in who's an expert in your area and do the organizing; some of their brand will rub off on you. Blog. Write articles. Show people how great you are – don't tell them.'

How long does it take?

Just as it takes a long time to create bad perceptions, erasing them can't be done overnight.

What if there are failings from your past that are not so easy to consign to history? Mr Olins says you can't deal with problems by ignoring them – if you worked for a failed bank, being upfront about it may help your brand recover but pretending it never happened won't. But there are limits to what a rebranding can achieve. There is the so-called 'career-limiting move' – a mistake so egregious, you never recover. 'Some events are so strong you can't dissociate yourself from them,' says Mr Fletcher. 'In this case, you need to move jobs. That's the best rebranding opportunity of all.'

Performing well in meetings

Meetings are often a microcosm of the world of work. In these gatherings, decisions are made, office politics played out and reputations burnished or tarnished. How do you ensure that you come across as best you can?

How do I get my point across?

First, prepare what you want to say beforehand. This is not just to help you clarify your thoughts but also because you should be ready for people to disagree with you – even if they do so just for the sake of looking clever in front of others. Meetings are not meant to be hostile occasions but it helps to think of them as debates. Practising beforehand will help you avoid being outmanoeuvred.

Second, select the right time to make your point. 'Don't rush in until you know the lie of the land,' says Professor Nigel Nicholson of London Business School.

Try to speak to everyone in the meeting, not just the chairperson. 'You should keep your voice grounded [in terms of pitch],' adds Nick Smallman, managing director of Working Voices, a personal impact consultancy. 'It makes you more credible.'

Get your message across succinctly and in sober language and resist the urge to show off; if you only need 30 seconds, only take 30 seconds. It is far better to have a reputation for being a wise person of few words than one for someone who prizes quantity over quality.

Finally, frame your position as something that is in everyone's interest rather than just your own.

How should I respond to other people's points?

If you do disagree with someone else, base your argument on cool logic, not hot emotion. Ask questions rather than reject things outright. This is an extension of good etiquette – it is all about engaging with those around you. 'Show an interest in your colleagues,' says Professor Nicholson. 'People are flattered when others take an interest.'

Body language helps here. 'People who are interested will focus on the speaker with their eyes and sit forward,' says Mr Smallman. 'They nod. They look engaged.'

Professor Nicholson agrees: 'People get so wrapped up in their own agendas – showing empathy is very important and often helps you get the outcome you want.'

What if you are chairing the meeting?

Strong leadership is not usually called for. 'If you're the chair, you should be someone who can see the subtext as well as the text,' explains Professor Nicholson. 'You want to ensure the job gets done and that everyone leaves the room feeling OK.'

This means nudging those who tend towards loquacity towards their points, helping those who shrink back to find their voices, making those who disagree find common ground. 'A good meeting should feel like a forum where everyone's voice can be heard,' says Mr Smallman.

What about the end?

Overrunning is one of the biggest complaints and if you are the chair, one of the easiest wins for you is to guide things to a timely end. Just because a meeting has been scheduled for an hour, it does not mean it needs to take an hour. If you manage to cover all the necessary ground in 30 minutes, call the meeting to an early finish. You will be giving everyone half an hour of their lives back, and they will be grateful for that.

Professional awards

It's a running joke that every industry has its Oscars. But how valuable is winning a gong in your industry? And what should you do if you are honoured in this way?

Do awards really make you stand out?

'They differentiate you from other people and act as a kind of third-party endorsement, which is very valuable in today's tough jobs market,' says Catherine Kaputa, a New York-based personal branding expert. 'People like things that are easy to latch on to and remember, so they'll say: "Oh, he or she won an award for that." It can become a kind of recommendation.'

Alan Young, creative director at St Luke's, the London advertising agency, adds: 'In creative circles, there's a huge desire for peer group recognition and having produced award-winning work will certainly keep you employable and may boost your earning power.'

Are all awards equal?

No. For a start, awards are much more important and prevalent in some sectors than others. Second, the money-making potential for the people behind the awards (usually via pricey ceremonies and high entry fees) means there are plenty of less credible schemes out there. So you need to do your research.

'There are awards that aren't worth the paper they're written on and to be encouraged by them is a road to confusion,' warns Ben Williams, a business psychologist in Edinburgh. Indeed, having a low-rent award might even tarnish your personal brand by making you look like an easily impressed sucker.

Should I advertise my awards?

'You need to weave it into your personal narrative rather than shout about it,' says Ms Kaputa. 'You don't want to seem arrogant. If a third party brings it up, that's great.'

Equally, you should not campaign too hard to be entered for awards. It is fine to promote yourself, but do not appear to be overly self-promoting or, worse, deluded. Stevan Rolls, human resources director of the professional services firm Deloitte, says that for those who win them, an award is usually just the icing on the cake:

'The important thing to remember is that…they tend to be good anyway – that's what really drives their career progression.'

Are there other benefits?

Whether or not you win, awards can still be a powerful incentive to raise your game. 'Being in the running for an award can give you a goal to work towards and act as a motivator,' says Ms Kaputa. 'There's a human need to show how good we are, particularly if we're ambitious.'

Awards can also have wider implications for the organization as a whole. 'When an individual or a team wins an award, it says something about us as a firm,' says Mr Rolls. 'Everyone feels good.'

Mr Williams says they can also help put training and development on the agenda.

Are there any pitfalls to watch out for?

'If you become too fixated on them and don't win, you can be crushed,' says Mr Young. He adds that too narrow a focus on sectoral prizes can be harmful in other ways, too. 'In our industry, the ads that win awards are often the crazy, weird showy things that slip through the net. Having an award-winning agenda can often create a lot of tension with the clients you're working with.'

How to make a good first impression

As the saying goes, you never get a a second chance to make a first impression. So whether it is your first day in a role, a job interview or just a meeting with a new client, how do you make one that counts?

Why are first impressions so important?

Corinne Mills, managing director of Personal Career Management, explains that people do not just hold on to first impressions, they also actively seek to reinforce them. 'If you make a good first impression, people will look for the best in you. If you make a bad or indifferent first impression, you have to work so much harder afterwards.'

Louise Mowbray, a personal branding consultant, agrees: 'If you make a bad first impression, it's very difficult to reverse – it can take around 100 directly opposing experiences to change that opinion.'

How should I prepare?

'It's all visual to start off with,' says Ms Mills. 'You need to look contemporary and appropriate – if you're starting a new job, then this is the time to get a new suit and a new haircut. If you look up-to-date, others will believe that your ideas and thinking are up-to-date; people do make these assumptions.'

Ms Mowbray says you need to ensure you are physically relaxed. 'Body language doesn't lie: ensure you're relaxed when you meet someone – and make sure you don't have to run to meetings.'

How should I behave?

'Treat people as though they are your peers,' advises Ms Mills. 'Don't be too deferential or cocky. Have a sense of self.'

Nick Smallman, founder of Working Voices, a communication and presentation skills consultancy, says you should put the other person at ease, speak in a level, clear voice, be open and confident, ask questions and listen – it is a truism that most people's favourite topic is themselves.

What are the main pitfalls?

You need to be authentic. Unrealistic embellishments will not help your confidence and can create future problems. 'Don't put yourself in a position where you're forever having to cover up,' says Ms Mowbray.

Finally, remember that good manners go a long way – so do not take mobile phone calls unless you absolutely have to.

What if things are going badly?

'It's worth asking the other person,' says Ms Mills. 'Say something like, "Is this a bad time for you?" or "Am I missing something?" '

This, she explains, shows both confidence and sensitivity. 'I had a client who had a job interview with a chief executive who barely looked at him. After a while, he asked, "Is something wrong?" and the guy said, "Didn't anyone tell you before you came in? My father just died." After that, the interview actually went okay and he got the job.'

How do I cement a good first impression?

'Once you've made a good first impression, you should try and find a way to show that you can produce,' says Mr Smallman. 'If you say you will e-mail someone a useful website or some information, do it the following morning. That way, they'll believe that you deliver.' Not least, of course, because the terrific first impression you made means they will be looking for the good points in you anyway.

Manners at work

Stereotypically, the cut-throat world of business favours the aggressive, the abrasive and the generally Type A. But is there room for good manners or do they just make you look like a pushover?

What good are manners at work?

Ben Williams, Edinburgh-based chartered psychologist, says that polite workplaces tend to retain staff longer, run more smoothly and be less prone to backbiting and internal sabotage. 'If you fail to show respect to people, their commitment drops and the quality of their work drops,' he says. 'They're less willing to go the extra mile for you.'

William Hanson, a Manchester-based etiquette consultant, says that as you climb the corporate ladder and are asked to be a representative of your company, manners become increasingly important. 'We're often called in to improve people's social skills when they've taken up a new role.'

What should I do?

Jacqueline Whitmore, an etiquette expert based in Palm Beach, Florida, says even simple good manners can go a long way. 'A lot of people come to work and don't even say good morning to their co-workers. Just by doing that, you can start to set the tone.'

She says a major source of unmannerliness in the modern workplace is technology. 'If you're in a meeting, don't sit there tapping away on a BlackBerry.'

Similarly, you should tell people off in private (and perhaps praise them in public); frame things the right way; use 'I' statements, not 'you' statements; and try to understand what your co-workers are sensitive to.

'No one gets up and decides to be rude,' she says. 'But people don't know what they don't know. You need to solicit feedback from colleagues. Or if you're going abroad on business, buy a few books on the country or read a few websites.'

What do I get out of it?

'If you're kind and well mannered it becomes part of your personal brand and who you are,' says Ms Whitmore. 'Equally rudeness can become part of your brand.'

Polite people are easier to get on with, they make better first impressions and others are more likely to think well of them, regardless of how they actually perform; they are also likely to be more confident as they'll know how to behave.

Does being polite make me a pushover?

No, says Mr Hanson – but you have to be emotionally intelligent. 'Ideally you should be polite but someone your colleagues know not to mess with.'

Mr Williams takes a similar line. 'You can be very assertive and still be courteous. If you lower your standards, you just let yourself down, whereas if you stay polite, it keeps you in the powerful position.'

Are there any easy wins?

'It's not rocket science but a bad handshake makes a very bad impression,' says Mr Hanson.

Other easy wins include not taking phone calls when you're talking to someone, looking at people when you talk to them, and dressing appropriately, even if it means being occasionally overdressed.

Delivering presentations

For many people, making a presentation is one of the most terrifying parts of working life. But, done well, presentations can also be a good opportunity to shine and impress people far beyond your immediate team.

Why are presentations important?

'Presentations are extraordinarily good for your reputation if you do them properly,' says Nick Smallman, managing director of Working Voices, communication and presentation skills consultancy. 'It's like doing your own PR and it's a chance for more people to see what is good about you. Good presenters get promoted.'

The problem, says Bob Etherington, author of *Presentation Skills for Quivering Wrecks*, is that most people are not very good at them. 'Most speakers want to get off the stage and most audiences want to get out of the room. If you can do a half-decent job, you're head and shoulders above the rest,' he says.

How should I prepare?

'Research your audience so you get the message right for them,' says Mr Smallman.

When you give your presentation, you should not be delivering it for the first time. Rehearse in front of colleagues and family, or by using a video camera rather than a mirror. You should not need a script – though cue cards are usually acceptable.

How do I deal with nerves?

'Imagine doing the presentation beforehand,' says Ben Williams, Edinburgh-based business psychologist. 'Take yourself through the whole movie and picture the audience responding really well. When you go along on the day, it'll be like déjà-vu.'

What makes a good presentation?

'A good presentation should be a conversation with your audience,' says Mr Smallman. 'It should feel intimate, even if it's 200 people.'

In fact, it makes good sense to think of your audience as lots of groups of a few people rather than a monolithic bloc. You need to start with a strong opening: wake people up and intrigue them; you can even antagonize them a bit if it gets their attention.

Do not try to pack too much in, warns Mr Etherington. 'Unless you're a real pro, aim to get one or two major points across,' he says.

Remember that people learn by repetition. Dry facts, he explains, are not persuasive, 'but people love stories and a bit of theatre – when Khrushchev banged his shoe at the UN, it was pre-prepared; and we once paid an actor to interrupt. Prod people every 30 seconds or so to keep them with you.'

You need a big finish too, says Mr Etherington. 'It's actually quite easy to manipulate an audience into applause,' he says. 'It's the rhythm. Deliver three final points in a low, calm voice standing still, then at the big moment become animated and raise your voice.'

What about PowerPoint?

'The odd picture or graph can work well but complex slides are suicide,' says Mr Smallman.

Bullet points are dreadful too, as is reading from slides. Many people make the mistake of spending eight hours on their PowerPoint presentation and half an hour on what they are going to say. This is back to front: PowerPoint should be a sparingly used visual aid, not a crutch.

Coping with being seen as too young

Ageism is usually an obstacle faced by older people. But if you are rising up the ranks fast, how do you deal with people who think you are too young for the job?

How do I cope with this issue in interviews?

'Focus on your experience,' says Isabelle Ratinaud, marketing director of the recruitment site Monster. 'You might have a short CV in terms of time but have accomplished a lot, so talk about quantifiable results and try to link these to business performance.'

How do I approach the job?

'Senior younger people often feel they have to prove their skills,' says Cary Cooper, professor of organizational psychology at Lancaster University. 'They think: "I'm 20 years younger and these older people will resent me – I need to show them I'm worth this role." They would be far better off engaging with them and listening.'

Elizabeth Bacchus, a career coach, says: 'People worry that they won't be taken seriously. One of the key things is to be confident. Show you can work with colleagues and make sure you contribute to discussions. Remember some of the advantages of youth are energy, enthusiasm and a fresh perspective – and make sure you don't lose your sense of self. You're employed to bring something you have to the table, so you shouldn't act like everyone else.'

What about managing a team?

Use your emotional intelligence and remember that everyone likes to be listened to. 'You will often need to be a bit of a chameleon,' says Ms Bacchus.

'You need to respect people's experience and ask for advice,' adds Professor Cooper. 'But if you ask for advice, you must use it where you feel it's relevant. If you don't, this will backfire.'

Help those you manage to learn new skills and develop their own careers, drawing on the experience of older members if possible. Ms Ratinaud says perhaps the single best thing you can do is to prove yourself: 'People will respect you if you deliver great results and advance the team's reputation.'

How do I defuse obvious prejudices?

'If you look very young, you might try to ensure you dress appropriately and soberly,' says Ms Ratinaud, noting that young men sometimes wear poorly fitting suits and younger women can be too creative with their attire. 'Present yourself as mature in terms of voice and gestures too.'

What about people who still undermine you?

'If someone makes a cutting comment, try to turn it into a positive,' says Ms Bacchus. 'Say: "I don't know much about that – what can I learn from you?"'

However, Professor Cooper adds: 'With some, you will never connect. They will be putting you down the whole time. You can't ignore it or pussyfoot around it because they will make it impossible for you to do your job. Rather, you have to confront it head on and have a meeting where you get it out. Don't be personal but explain the reality – that they need to get over it because you are now their boss.'

Writing for work

What we write at work forms an important part of how we are perceived. Yet many people barely think about what they have committed to permanence and leave behind a record of difficult-to-decipher, error-strewn, jargon-riddled prose.

How important is written communication?

'Most people in business spend a lot of time writing documents or if they're more senior, reading them,' says Neil Taylor, of The Writer, the business language consultancy. 'If you're the author, your bid might be competing with six other bids that are essentially the same – or you might write a document for the board three times a year. How you write it makes a huge difference.'

Your written output helps shape your reputation, says Robert Myatt, a director at Kaisen, the business psychologists. 'In an age where e-mails are cc'd to hundreds of people it's a real chance to stand out.'

Mr Taylor adds that a lot of writing is actually a sales pitch. 'You're selling an idea, your services or even your personality.'

What are the most common problems and how do I address them?

'People get into a speed habit,' says Stephen Lloyd, a business writing consultant. 'I always say, "You should think, write and review," but often people just do the writing.' Mr Lloyd says this is particularly true of e-mails. 'Because they are often used for informal communication, people treat them informally. But an e-mail can be a very important business document. Taking a little more time over what you write often saves time in the long run.'

Mr Taylor says the desire to sound professional and businesslike can also lead to poor writing. 'People forget they're people. They make their writing complex and dense because they feel it's expected of them. It's not. Good writing is short, engaging and gets the point over.'

While concision and clarity should always be the goal, they do of course vary between industries. 'In a retail environment, you probably want to be pithy and succinct and you might be able to get away with using a lot of abbreviations – anything too long might be seen as verbose,' Mr Myatt says. 'In a law firm, however, people may take huge pride in the quality of their written communications.'

What about jargon?

'Jargon doesn't help anyone – it's putting up a barrier and often looks like you're hiding an inability to communicate clearly,' Mr Lloyd says.

There is nothing wrong with using the language of your business, but it should be used to clarify rather than obfuscate. As Warren Buffet states in the preface to *A Plain English Handbook: How to Create Clear SEC Disclosure Documents*: 'Write [in plain English] as this handbook instructs you and you will be amazed at how much smarter your readers will think you have become.'

He also offers this tip: 'When writing Berkshire Hathaway's annual report, I pretend that I'm talking to my sisters... They will understand plain English, but jargon may puzzle them.'

Are there some things I should never write?

The internet is littered with specific examples of this, but a good workaday rule is never to write in anger. 'Don't e-mail if you feel emotional,' Mr Myatt says, 'Write it by all means, but don't send it.'

How to blow your own trumpet

We have long been told that we are the CEOs of our own careers. But many people still struggle to be their own marketing director. So how do you promote yourself without coming across as self-promoting?

Why do I need to promote myself?

'It's no longer enough to be good at your job,' says Lesley Everett, founder of Walking Tall, a personal branding consultancy. 'You need to promote yourself and take an entrepreneurial approach to your career – with your behaviour, attitude and visibility.'

She argues that in many sectors and countries, reticence and self-deprecation have given way to an altogether more proactive approach to self-promotion. 'People are very busy and love clarity,' she says. 'If you can tell them what you really bring to the table they'll thank you for it.'

How do I get it right?

There are two essential ingredients. First is authenticity: your message needs to reflect the real you. 'It's like a signature dish,' says Jennifer Holloway, founder of executive coaching company Spark. 'You need to look at the ingredients that make you different and combine them in the best possible way.' Second, she says: 'Blow your trumpet at a volume that suits you. You need to be comfortable with it.'

Gregarious people can often get away with being a bit over the top, but others can struggle. 'The first time you try increasing the volume, you may feel uncomfortable, but if it suits you, you'll get used to it,' she says. 'One guy I work with won't even say he's a marketing director because he thinks the term "director" is too showy. We've agreed he'll say he's "responsible for marketing", which is a step forward for him.'

Do I give everyone the same message?

'Your message needs to be consistent, but it can be multilayered so you can tailor it to your audience,' says Ms Everett. You should be showing different facets of 'Brand You' to different people based on what they need.

Is it all about talking myself up?

Often, it is just about making yourself easy to remember – in a good way. It can be quite subtle – everything from your voicemail message (never say 'Sorry') to how you dress to not prefixing your suggestions with 'You'll probably hate this but...'.

Putting yourself up as a spokesperson, learning to be a good public speaker, blogging and using social media are all good means of self-promotion. Perhaps the best way, however, is to get other people to talk you up. 'Become a good networker,' says Geraldine Gallacher of the Executive Coaching Consultancy. 'The more people you know, the more influence you have.' And, she adds, 'getting your clients to sing your praises for you' is a great way to reap brownie points.

What about cultural differences?

Broadly speaking, Americans are much more forward about putting themselves forward than Europeans and Asians. But it is very contextual. 'The American approach in Germany would be too much,' says Ms Everett, 'but in the United States, it comes across as very positive.'

Similarly, in sales-based roles, a high degree of self-promotion is often expected, but the same approach in professional services might come across as rather strange.

Managing your online presence

You should expect prospective employers to research you using Google, LinkedIn and Facebook. So how do you ensure your online persona is someone they would want to employ?

Do I have to have an online presence?

'Your online profile is becoming increasingly hard to ignore,' says Sid Barnes, executive director at IT recruitment specialists Computer

People. Rather than worrying about it, he says, 'You should view this as an opportunity to show yourself in the best possible light. An online profile can say so much more than a two-page CV and include connections and recommendations.'

Jennifer Holloway of personal branding consultancy Spark adds: 'It amazes me how many people don't have an online presence. People like to Google you.'

Where should I start?

'I'd highly recommend putting your profile on LinkedIn,' says social media strategist Krishna De. 'When people search, results from LinkedIn come up high in results. When you're writing your profile think about the terms people search for.'

Ms Holloway adds: 'Join LinkedIn groups to do with your areas of expertise and contribute to the discussion.'

Can I go beyond obvious social networking sites?

'You could use a blog to talk about your career and related subjects you're interested in,' says Ms De. 'Build up followers and a group of people. You can tweet about work and you can also put slide presentations you've made online with sites like Slideshare.'

As well as actively putting material online, you can also check what is being said about you using Google alerts. If something bad is written about you, says Ms Holloway, a good remedy is to flood the web with more positive comment.

What about the personal side of things?

Mr Barnes says that it may help to think of LinkedIn as your professional reputation and Facebook as your social reputation.

'On the social side, potential employers and recruiters like to see how people come across in the world and what their convictions and passions are,' he says. 'It gives a better idea of what a candidate's about. But you need to be careful. No one needs to know you can down 20 Sambuca shots or see compromising photos of you. You need to weigh up what portrays you as a good all-rounder, but not go too far.'

With Facebook it is worth looking at your privacy settings – and having a quiet word with friends who are tagging you in inappropriate photos.

Be strategic and cautious in your linking

'Think about quality not quantity,' says Mr Barnes. 'For most people much more than 300 LinkedIn connections just suggests you collect connections.'

Ms Holloway adds that you need to be careful about cross-linking networks: 'I've seen people make offensive tweets, forgetting that they'll then appear on their LinkedIn pages.'

Showcasing your qualifications

You have been to business school and graduated with an MBA. But what is the best way to exploit your qualification? Who do you tell about it and what do you say to them? And, perhaps most important, how do you do so without coming across as boastful, smug or arrogant?

Where does it belong when applying for jobs?

Julia Zupko, director of career management at Chicago Booth Business School, says that in interview situations it is particularly important to highlight your experiences and then tie these to your MBA. 'Part of what an MBA provides is new ways of thinking. So start with the skills and experience and then bring in your MBA. Offer credible examples of how you put your MBA to work and how it makes you more effective.'

When it comes to your CV, Nigel Parslow, UK managing director of executive search firm Harvey Nash, says you should bring it to the fore. 'Get it out there in bold and state the school you went to. Mention it in the covering letter and don't hide it down with qualifications you gained 12 years ago.'

Are there any other key points I should make?

Not all MBAs are created equal. 'Top schools have a great deal of credibility,' says Mr Parslow. 'Make sure you tell people where you went.'

If you were sponsored to do your MBA or if you did it while working, then draw particular attention to this. These kinds of factors are likely to count in your favour.

How do you handle people who are sniffy about MBAs?

Some people, especially older or entrepreneurial types, can be dismissive of MBAs, believing you cannot learn about business in a classroom. Mr Parslow says that if someone takes this line 'bat it back. Explain that you were doing very well but that you wanted to increase the breadth of your knowledge and gain new tools. You can add that you know it's not a prerequisite for success but that you believe it's going to help.'

Personal branding expert Louise Mowbray says that if you have done an MBA you should be aiming at those who appreciate them. 'You have to understand that you can't be all things to all people. Everything you do in your career needs to be targeted.'

Should I alter my approach for different fields?

In the United States and in sectors such as consultancy and finance, an MBA is often what Ms Zupko calls 'a de facto entry point' and you will be expected to shout about it. But the opposite does not necessarily hold in Europe and Asia and in sectors where MBAs are a less common currency. On the one hand, they can be more of a positive differentiator, but on the other they may mean little and it can be wiser to be more nuanced.

Should I put MBA on my business card?

This is a tough one. Ms Zupko says probably not. 'Putting MBA on your business card could be seen as pretentious and a bit unprofessional.'

But Ms Mowbray says you should. 'Obviously, you need to handle it carefully, but I think as long as it's relevant to your audience, you should put it on.'

In any case, you should not have more letters after your name than there are in your name.

How to be an iconoclast

We're forever being told by everyone – from management gurus to Apple's old advertising campaign – that we need to think differently in order to stand out. And there is no doubt that many at the top in their fields have got there by defying conventional wisdom. But can you really try to become an iconoclast?

Is standing out good?

'Most organizations are actually very conservative, even if they say they want risk-takers,' says Gregory Berns, professor of neuro-economics at Emory University and author of *Iconoclast: A Neuro-scientist Reveals How to Think Differently*. And different is not always better, says Octavius Black, founder of performance consultancy the Mind Gym. 'You don't want to be the prickly rebel that no one likes. You want to be the creative force who drives everyone to think differently.'

Can I train myself to think differently?

Professor Berns says that if you are in the same environment with the same people every day, you're unlikely to be having radical ideas. 'The easiest way to create new ideas and remix old ones is to put yourself in situations you've never been in before,' he explains. 'Travel seems very effective, as long as you don't do it all the time.

Coming into contact with people and cultures that are very different forces you to think in ways that are different.'

He suggests asking your company to move you to different tasks or areas of the business. Continuing education works well too, especially if in new areas, 'Most of my new ideas come from outside my field,' he says.

Mr Black says that looking differently at the familiar can work too: 'Try to look at an everyday situation through the eyes of someone else – or write something in the style of someone else.' He adds that much of the process is getting into the right frame of mind: 'Treat everything as a stimulus for the next idea,' he says.

How do I get the message out?

There is no point in having great, radical ideas if you keep them to yourself. However, says Professor Berns, communicating them can be difficult, especially in large organizations: 'A lot of it boils down to fear of looking stupid in front of a group.'

Two of the best things you can do, he says, are to conquer your fear of public speaking and to enlist the support of a colleague. He adds that people who think differently may not necessarily have great social skills. 'In this case, it's completely reasonable to partner with people,' he says.

Mr Black says the best iconoclasts encourage those around them: 'Embrace others' new ideas. People are far more likely to support you if you're enthusiastic about them.'

Are there any pitfalls?

Louise Mowbray, personal branding consultant, warns against in-authenticity. 'You can't wear a three-piece suit if your attitude is messed-up jeans. A lot of it is having the courage to be yourself. That can be very difficult, especially if you're young.' She adds that you should not spread yourself too thinly either: successful people tend to focus on doing one thing brilliantly.

Finally, she suggests, you need to be consistent. Repetition is the key to changing people's perceptions.

How to deal with being put on the spot

Being put in an awkward position, especially in meetings, is uncomfortable but it happens all the time – and may be either unintentional or malicious. So how should you react?

What should my immediate reaction be?

Stay calm. 'Other people can only put you on the spot if you let them,' says Mike Leibling, author of *How People Tick*. 'People are conditioned in school and university, where you get prizes for coming up with the right answer quickly, so they feel they have to put their hand up. At work you're more likely to be rewarded for asking smart questions.'

Nick Smallman, managing director of Working Voices, a consultancy that specializes in interpersonal skills, says: 'The most important thing is that you don't have to panic and think of an answer. Take your time and relax.'

How should I respond?

'If you don't know the full answer don't try and bluff your way out of it,' says Mr Smallman. 'Tell them what you know and what you don't know. Be clear and direct.' You could also play for time or ask the questioner what they might do in the situation.

Mr Leibling suggests offering a firm, reasonable response: 'Say: "I need to give you an answer you can rely on, so let me go away and have a think."'

You can also use strategies to leave the awkward moment behind – for example, say you have not been briefed on the issue and move on. 'The worst kind of response is an apology where you just ramble on and everyone is thinking, "Shut up already,"' Mr Leibling concludes.

Should matters escalate, remain calm, as this strengthens your hand. Try saying something such as: 'I clearly misunderstood you.

Can we discuss this later?' A final option is to excuse yourself to get some breathing space.

Can I prepare?

Ben Williams, Edinburgh-based corporate psychologist, advises working on skills with colleagues. 'Ask them for quick-fire questions. Get people to ambush you and see if you can handle it. Politicians practise this sort of thing all the time.' Indeed, a quick-draw response can burnish your reputation.

What if it is malicious?

There are a number of options. Mr Smallman says: 'You can just ask the person, "Why do you want to know?" – which, in this instance, is a kind of "When did you stop beating your wife?" type question. You can get on the front foot.' Mr Williams suggests making light of the question, although there is a chance that this approach could make you an enemy.

Bear in mind, though, that what appears to be malice may have another cause. You might be put on the spot in order to throw someone such as a client a lifeline, says Mr Leibling. It might also be a one-off, where a colleague feels you should face a tough question because they have. In this case, you should let it go.

How do I ensure it doesn't become a pattern?

First deal with the situation privately, and in a mature, reasoned way. Usually, noting it is enough. If it's part of a pattern, though, it needs to be addressed. Mr Leibling advises: 'Say, "I feel you're doing this maliciously. The person may not realize they're doing it, and eight times out of ten people will be mortified. You may want to check that other colleagues feel the same way beforehand.'

If this does not work, you have two options. One is to tell the person you will not be put in this position again. The second option – a rather more diplomatic approach – is to say something like: 'We all seem to misunderstand you. Perhaps you could make this clearer.'

Dressing to impress

What to wear at work is often treated as rather frivolous. But neglecting your appearance and having an inattention to detail can hold you back in the office.

How important is how you dress?

'A lot of people don't think it matters,' says Nicola Bunting of La Vita Nuova, a personal and executive coaching company. 'But they're sadly mistaken. It really is worth educating yourself about what works for you.'

Lesley Everett, founder of Walking Tall personal branding consultancy, adds: 'People do judge. James Laver [the fashion historian] said "clothes … are the furniture of the mind made visible". Never underestimate how much they can help you. People are always being overlooked because they don't look the part.'

What's appropriate for my workplace?

'Know the rules in your game,' says Peter York, cultural commentator and author of *The Official Sloane Ranger Handbook*. 'You want to know what is considered top form in your sector and in the associated social world, as if you're ambitious you'll be socializing with work. What looks dull in adland might look very good in the civil service.'

Mr York adds that it is fine to break the rules, just 'not accidentally'.

How do I differentiate myself?

Ms Bunting says: 'Express yourself in an aspirational way. The trick is to dress up – one or two levels above your current role.'

For both sexes, but especially men, bespoke tailoring is worth investing in. 'The difference,' says Ms Bunting, 'is night and day.' Similarly accessories can do a great deal: ties, cufflinks, jewellery and watches can all make an outfit. 'People often let themselves down with poor-quality details. But good details become who you are,' she says.

What about dress-down days and smart casual?

The trick is to take smart casual very seriously and buy the right kit. 'If you're not wearing a tie, don't use a shirt made for a tie,' says Mr York.

Ms Everett adds: 'A huge mistake men make is to do smart casual dress with smart formal shoes. Or they just wear old chinos and polo shirts. For summer, you need to look at lightweight fabrics such as linens and silks. A dress-down day isn't a slob day.'

What should I watch out for?

Understand what makes you look good. A pink shirt or blouse goes well with dark skin, far less so with a pale complexion. If you don't have a clue, seek advice from stylists or personal shoppers. And remember, people will always notice stains, tears and dirt.

'You need to be authentic,' adds Ms Everett. 'You shouldn't dress as someone you're not.'

How do I tell a colleague that their dress sense is letting them down?

'Encourage a culture of feedback and communication,' says Ms Everett. 'It's easier if there is a dress code but if there isn't, the best thing to tell them is: "Your image is getting in the way of your true qualities and abilities."'

Making body language work

The majority of communication is non-verbal. But how do you make sure your workplace body language is on message?

How important is body language?

'We're very influenced by non-verbal communication,' says Joe Navarro, author of *What Every Body is Saying: An ex-FBI Agent's*

Guide to Speed-reading People. If you look at presidential debates, the body language of the candidates is often what people recall most. 'They remember their mannerisms and how they looked. In the workplace a lack of social intelligence is what keeps a lot of people from climbing the ladder,' he says.

Elizabeth Kuhnke, an executive coach and body language expert, says: 'It is a very important part of relationship building. Establish that rapport and people will follow your lead; you control the emotional agenda. Remember that body language existed before language.'

What are some of the basics?

'The real tip is to convey confidence,' says Ben Williams, corporate psychologist. 'Think back to the times when you've been successful and felt good when you want to project confidence.' General tips, Mr Williams explains, include standing up straight, smooth gestures, nodding and smiling without being obsequious and keeping your hands below your elbows. You should also be aware of your tics such as fiddling with jewellery, pens and hair, and practise not doing them, as they can be very distracting and undermine your message.

The same is true of some natural emotional responses, says Ms Kuhnke. 'If you feel moist eyed, look up towards where the wall and the ceiling meet. It will make you appear thoughtful. If you think you're about to explode, breathe deeply and take the air right down. It slows you down. Being emotionally controlled is a matter of practice and awareness.'

However, says Mr Navarro, keeping your real feelings on a short leash is not always desirable. 'There are times when you should let emotions show. Leaders should be seen to be empathetic, especially when times are difficult.' Finally, he adds, it is not just what you do, it's how fast you do it. 'If you go to see people quickly when you enter a room, it multiplies positive feelings.'

What about other people's body language?

'You need to be aware and read people,' says Ms Kuhnke. 'If they're flushing, then something you've said has affected them deeply. Open eyes are a "Tell me more" expression. But if their head is on you while their body is turned away, they're just being polite. Tailor your responses appropriately.'

Mr Williams says that you have to be a bit careful about ascribing exact meanings to single gestures. 'Touching your nose can mean you're telling a lie or it can mean that your nose is itching.'

Rather, says Ms Kuhnke, you want to watch out for clusters of gestures: 'Arms crossed, peering over glasses and thinned lips probably means someone is closed off.'

Mr Navarro says that good, empathetic leaders will act on body language. 'If you're in a meeting and you see uncomfortable behaviour, such as wringing of hands, ask people if everything is all right, rather than just ploughing on.'

Does it vary with culture?

There are enormous differences between West and the East and North and South, says Mr Navarro and you need to pick up on them. 'If it's your third visit to Bogotá, you should be hugging, not shaking hands. You need to communicate that, culturally speaking, you get it.' Remember too that there are some sectoral differences. In law, for instance, people tend to be cool, calm and reserved, while in the creative sectors being more animated might be expected.

Chapter Six
Business or pleasure?

Humour in the workplace

One of the easiest ways to endear yourself to someone is to make them laugh. So it is no surprise that showing a little humour in the workplace can advance your career. But how do you tread the fine line between being funny and being a joke?

How can being funny help my career?

'Knowing when to be funny shows people that you are open, likeable and not some robotic technocrat,' says Cary Cooper, professor of organizational psychology at Lancaster University. 'If you watch them, many CEOs know just when to use humour.'

Humour is also an excellent way of defusing awkward situations and influencing people. Once you have disarmed your listeners with humour, they are much more likely to be receptive to new ideas and change.

Is workplace humour just about cracking jokes?

There is much more to it than that. 'It can be about finding a humorous take on things and dealing positively with anger, frustration and stress,' says Bill Rodgers of HumourUs, a workplace consultancy. 'It is about being fluid and flexible. Humour is a kind of oil that lubricates workplace transactions. It does everything from breaking the ice to improving productivity.'

How far is too far?

Obviously racist, sexist or homophobic is out. One person's idea of a joke can easily be another's idea of a discrimination suit.

Mr Rodgers says victimization is a no-go area. 'Humour has to be shared – you need to find a common denominator and it should never be focused on one person.'

The only person you should ever make jokes about is yourself. 'People with good social skills will understand when humour is appropriate and when it isn't,' says Professor Cooper. 'And if you use too much humour, others may think you have no substance.'

Is it possible to make yourself a funnier person?

'Humour is learned behaviour,' Mr Rodgers says. 'It's something we can all develop.' While there are people who bill themselves as 'humour coaches', much of being witty is about timing, confidence and the ability to observe and dissect a situation. So you may find improving your general presentation skills makes you funnier.

Does it translate across national boundaries?

Humour is so subjective that you can find an example to support any point of view on this. British journalist Toby Young has written about how 'high jinks' and practical jokes that had been considered funny in London went down like a lead balloon when he worked in New York.

Still, Professor Cooper believes Europe is developing something of a single market in humour: 'These days I think the same joke would work in Denmark, Spain and the UK.'

What about different industries?

Counter-intuitively, it can be easier to laugh about your job when it is no laughing matter. Certain sectors, such as medicine and the armed forces, have a reputation for a robust gallows humour, which works as a coping mechanism. But such *entre nous* jocularity can cause real problems if it reaches a wider audience. Even more than most jokes, they should never be committed to the leaky permanence of e-mail.

Socializing with colleagues

Going out with workmates after work is a grey area. It is not entirely work, but it is rarely pure pleasure either. Boundaries are blurred and etiquette can be uncertain. How do you make this ambiguous mix of the professional and personal work for you?

What do I get out of it?

'People who socialize with colleagues will have good chemistry with them and things are more likely to happen quickly,' says Sarah Sweetman, a business psychologist at Organizational Edge, the consultancy.

'If you know a bit about someone you'll understand their motivations, you're less likely to get frustrated with them and even if they don't give you what you want, you'll probably understand why.'

It is also a way of raising your profile and a form of participation. Farah Ramzan Golant, chief executive of AMV BBDO, the advertising agency, says: 'The culture of the agency [which is highly social] is very commercially important to us. Of course, you don't have to do anything, but if you don't socialize you won't be fully part of the culture. You do tend to notice who is visible and who isn't.'

Should I socialize with people above and below my grade?

While this can break down boundaries and help senior management stay in touch with what those at the coalface are thinking, there are plenty of situations where 'vertical socialization' makes things uncomfortable – the classic example is where the team wants to let off a bit of steam and their manager stays all evening.

'As a boss, it's good for your career if your team feel that you're human and approachable,' Ms Sweetman says. 'But you have to recognize that sometimes the best boss buys a couple of rounds and then heads home.'

What should I avoid?

'You need to maintain your dignity,' says Stephen Overell, associate director of The Work Foundation, a think-tank. 'Don't try too hard to impress and don't get too drunk. If you do embarrass yourself, either make efforts to redeem yourself or move on quietly.'

Socializing with colleagues should also be inclusive rather than cliquey. And you should be careful with gossip – there is a fine line between being a valued source of intelligence and a spreader of innuendo. Similarly, buttonholing a senior manager to complain about anything and everything is unlikely to do much for your career prospects.

Finally, work socializing has its practical limits. Well-balanced people need lives outside the office and going out with colleagues four times a week is hardly conducive to this. Staff should not feel pressured to attend every single event. 'Anything that smacks of organized fun will put people off,' adds Mr Overell. 'You need spontaneity.'

Can my colleagues be my friends?

The mistake many people make here is not realizing that, while spending eight hours a day together gives you a great deal in common, often it is all you have in common. 'Work relationships can be very intense, but you often don't sustain them once you leave,' Mr Overell says.

Ms Sweetman takes a similar line. 'Colleagues are not the same as friends,' she says. 'The rules are different and the stakes are different.'

Pro bono work

Pro bono work is usually thought of as the preserve of lawyers, but organizations as varied as advertising agencies and professional services firms also donate their staff's time to good causes – either for free or for reduced fees. Although employees should do pro bono work for selfless reasons, your good deeds can also be rewarded in terms of your career.

How does pro bono work add to my experience?

If you are relatively junior, it can be a very good way to step up. 'People who do pro bono work in the Accenture Development Partnerships (ADP) typically take on more senior roles than they would in big corporate roles,' says Royce Bell, a senior executive at the consultancy firm. 'You get to see a lot of nuts and bolts and it's very good to get outside the normal cosy corporate world. You'd think that someone who sets up an IT system in Chad would have a broader view than a person who has only worked in Fortune 200 companies.'

Six years ago, Maya Mehta, a senior associate at Clifford Chance, the law firm, set up the legal advice surgery for the Newham Asian Women's Project (NAWP) in London. 'It's a great way to sharpen your skills as a lawyer,' she says. 'Particularly with the high level of client contact and range of issues. As a trainee in Hong Kong, working with Filipino women who had been abused made me realize how much I could help others just by applying basic legal skills.'

What about opportunities for building relationships?

Pro bono work often brings together people from different parts of organizations who might not otherwise meet.

Phil Georgiadis, chairman of Walker Media, the London media agency, says it can cut through hierarchies, too. 'I'm about to do some work for Great Ormond Street Hospital and I'll enlist a couple of graduates to work with me – that'll be the account team. So suddenly you have a graduate who is reporting directly to the chairman, which is very rare,' he explains.

What about job satisfaction?

Using your professional skills in the service of good causes often adds a kind of ethical dimension to your career and can be very motivating. Ms Mehta says the inspiration for starting the NAWP pro bono scheme came about from reading about forced marriages and honour killings: 'It got to the point where I couldn't just turn the page. I wanted to do something about it.'

She says it is also one way of bridging the divide between Canary Wharf and the less privileged areas that surround it.

Pro bono work can be rewarding in other ways, too. Mr Georgiadis says you can be freer to be more creative with work done for charities: 'You often have the opportunity to do some really interesting marketing and [you have more leeway] than you might have with, say, a breakfast cereal.'

Mr Bell adds that ADP projects tend to be smaller and shorter than their corporate counterparts: 'It's much easier to see overall results and understand the positive effect of what you are doing.'

Are there any downsides?

Those who go on long-term schemes such as the ADP may be asked to take a reduced salary – although in the case of the ADP, if you're in Chad or Mongolia, even a reduced salary lets you live pretty well.

Outside activities

Talking to colleagues about what you do outside work can be a way of building rapport and adding to your personal brand. But are there some things you just shouldn't share?

What can it do for my career?

Talking about personal details in the office can be beneficial. Executive coach Ros Taylor says: 'I'm a great believer in the idea that you should bring yourself to work. So often people are one dimensional.'

Ms Taylor says that she has worked with buttoned-up solicitors who put on leathers at the weekend and ride Harley-Davidson motorcycles. Telling colleagues they do this humanizes them at the office. She adds that even if your pastime isn't for everyone, 'talking about it may be seen as standing up and being counted – it makes you look more confident'.

And letting your professional mask slip a little is no bad thing. 'I tell people, "I keep chickens and bees,"' says Jennifer Holloway of personal branding consultancy Spark. 'It's revealing and it gives them something to chat about.'

Alex Babic, a director at executive search firm DW Simpson, says: 'People at work know that I do stand-up comedy and voice-overs. It is a talking point and something that they remember you for.'

Are there limits to what is acceptable?

'It is a fine line,' says Ms Holloway. 'If you imagine a ladder that has the most professional you at the top and the very drunk you at the bottom, you need to decide what rung you want to reveal of yourself.'

She says that a further complication is a kind of 'social hygiene' factor that you get with pastimes such as hunting, religion and politics.

However, she adds that even potentially tricky activities can work in the right context. 'I worked with a hunter once and he was worried about saying he did that in a company report. But he went ahead and it turned out that a lot of his customers were farmers, so that was OK.'

Ms Taylor agrees. 'I've coached a CEO who collected death masks – he had one of James Joyce. Even strange pastimes can be quite consistent with who you are.'

However, you shouldn't become a pastime bore, as epitomized by the runner who tells colleagues about every training session. 'Don't inflict your hobbies on other people,' says Ms Taylor.

What if I don't want to divulge?

'There might be things you keep to yourself,' says Ms Holloway. 'But you should never actively lie, because doing so and getting caught will almost certainly be very embarrassing.'

For this reason, you may need to exercise caution on sites such as Facebook and Twitter. You should also keep some divide between the work and personal spheres – or there could be practical considerations.

Mr Babic says: 'I talk about my stand-up afterwards rather than announcing gigs beforehand. If I had a dozen colleagues watching, I could guarantee it would be the night I'd come across as a big angry, unfunny man wrestling with his demons, rather than a comic Lothario.'

Doing lunch

Business lunches may not be what they once were in the glory days of the 1980s, but they remain an invaluable way of connecting with clients, getting to know colleagues and improving working relationships. So, how do you make sure your working lunch works?

What is the point of a business lunch?

'Getting out of the office and spending some quality face time with a person away from distractions makes them feel special,' says Robin Jay, author of *The Art of the Business Lunch*. 'Unlike a meeting, sitting down and breaking bread with someone gives them a chance to open up, relax and make a real connection.'

The beauty of business lunches is that you do not go into them with a rigid agenda. 'Lunch is more discursive and an opportunity to talk more broadly,' says Arabella Ellis, a director at the Thinking

Partnership, a leadership consultancy. 'A business lunch turns a transactional relationship into something deeper.'

What restaurant should I choose?

'You need the right level of formality,' says Richard Harden of Harden's Guides, the restaurant review publisher. 'It needs to be somewhere that both you and your guest(s) will feel comfortable.'

Obviously what is right will vary according to the sector you work in and the seniority of your dining companions. Price point is also a complex issue. 'If you choose somewhere too expensive, your guests will feel obliged to you,' says Ms Ellis. 'This may make them feel uncomfortable and even angry. People know they don't get something for nothing.'

As well as location and dietary requirements, you should ask yourself if you are likely to be seen or overheard – and whether or not that matters.

How else can I prepare?

'Even if you have an excellent guidebook, a site visit is rarely wasted,' says Mr Harden. 'Familiarize yourself with the menus and look at the wine list and take a few notes so you'll be able to choose quickly and knowledgeably.' With many restaurants, you can now do this online.

'You should also tell people why you're inviting them to lunch,' says Ms Ellis. 'Is it to discuss strategy or to thank them for putting business your way? If you don't tell them, it can be awkward.'

If I am hosting a lunch, what is my role?

'If you're the host, you have to be very clear that you're in a leadership position,' says Ms Ellis. 'You should get there first and you should also realize that your guests look to you for guidance. On food and drink, you need to take the lead.'

Finally, lunch is a strange mix of business and pleasure – your guests may not be comfortable talking about their home lives. Here, you should follow their lead.

Are there any don'ts?

While it is acceptable to give your guest a few notes, it is bad form to bring a pitch document to lunch – and absolutely awful to pull out a laptop and do a PowerPoint presentation. You want your guest to feel comfortable, not like a captive audience.

Ms Jay says technology has no place at a restaurant table either: 'Turn your cellphone off and don't leave your BlackBerry on the table and check messages.'

The business breakfast

For many time-pressed, expenses-stretched businesspeople, breakfast really is the new lunch. But how do you make sure that the first meal of the day really works for you?

Why breakfast?

'Breakfast is far more time efficient than lunch,' says Robin Jay, author of *The Art of the Business Lunch*. 'It is very finite and there's a cut-off point. If you have to be in the office at 9.30, then you have to leave at 9. You don't need an exit strategy.' However, she adds: 'It is still much more than just a business meeting. You break bread together and that sharing is very important.'

Furthermore, while people sometimes feel guilty about lunching, they may actually feel virtuous about a business breakfast.

Are there any points of etiquette?

As breakfast is less formal, it can make for a good introductory meeting. If you are struggling to get into someone's diary for lunch, you might try breakfast instead. Cary Cooper, professor of organizational psychology at Lancaster University, says that people who view lunch as a hassle often see a breakfast as 'rather good fun'.

Because of the time constraints, punctuality is very important. 'Be a few minutes early,' advises Carole Stone, founder of the

TheStoneClub networking organization. 'Don't faff around, get the pleasantries over quickly and get down to business.'

If it is a larger breakfast with a speaker, ensure the table is cleared before they start. Being surrounded by half-eaten fried eggs can be off-putting.

What about the location and food?

Breakfast is considerably less formal than lunch, which means you have more leeway with venues. For instance, you might not have lunch in a Starbucks but for breakfast it would be fine. Indeed, if you have the facilities, your own office is a perfectly good place to have breakfast – and from the perspective of advancing your career, it will help if your boss catches you in the act.

Nonetheless, if you are choosing a restaurant, Ms Stone says you should select somewhere friendly and efficient: 'You don't want a place that's too fussy and formal where the service is time-consuming.'

Because breakfast has become quite a networking opportunity, she adds, popular breakfast restaurants such as the Wolseley in London can be a good option, too.

On the food front, breakfast menus have far fewer pitfalls than lunch menus do. 'I'd suggest something simple like scrambled eggs and bacon and toast,' says Ms Stone. 'If you're arranging it, you'd want to serve fruit and croissants, too. Most people don't want a heavy meal like a full English breakfast.'

When doesn't breakfast work?

'If you have a serious problem to discuss, breakfast probably isn't the right place as it means starting off your day on an unpleasant note,' says Professor Cooper.

He adds that you can also have too much of a good thing. 'Although I think working breakfasts are great, if you do them all the time, particularly if you're a parent, they can have work–life balance implications. You need to have family breakfasts too.'

And Ms Jay says that if you have a lot of business to discuss, lunch may still be preferable: 'A classic power lunch still needs to be a lunch.'

Extra-curricular activities

With thousands of employees in one place, large organizations can sometimes resemble university campuses. And like universities, they often offer a host of extra-curricular societies for those interested in arts and culture. But are these more than just a way to make the daily office grind more bearable?

Why are extra-curricular cultural societies popular when everyone is so busy with their day jobs?

Colin Tweedy, chief executive of Arts & Business, an organization that forges connections between commerce and culture, says these societies can fulfil a kind of spiritual need. 'Even people who consider themselves "masters of the universe" are looking for something else – and becoming more and more aware of life beyond long hours and big deals,' he says. There are more earthly benefits, too. 'It gives people the opportunity to develop new skills,' says Maria Bentley, global head of human resources and chair of the music club at UBS. The club has nearly 600 members in London who put on concerts and may even be found playing the piano in the company's foyer. 'Putting together a performance is like running a mini-business and an experience they might not otherwise get. If you can take a half-hour or an hour off to perform music, you'll probably perform better in your role.'

Are these activities a good way to network?

Matt Farrington, a law student who will join Allen & Overy in September, sang the part of Tamino in the firm's performance of *The Magic Flute* at the Glyndebourne opera house last month. 'It was a great musical experience and also a very good way of meeting people and learning about the company culture,' he says. 'There's a real cross-section of the firm and you get a lot of opportunities to chat informally with senior partners, which is not something normally afforded to junior employees.' Ms Bentley takes a similar line: 'Those who sit on the music club committee get exposure to senior management.' It is also a way of seeing a different side of those you work with. 'It's an activity beyond your regular day job that you do with your colleagues and can add another dimension to existing relationships.'

How about raising your profile?

It is a good way to become a spokesperson and helps to differentiate you in the same way as such activities do at university. 'In an age when everyone has three As and a double first, an interest in the arts can give you an edge,' says Mr Tweedy. He adds that it is very much in the interests of the business, too – a lot of companies support these activities partly to attract the best staff. 'Having staff involvement in the arts can add a hip and stylish edge to an organization and can help humanize an organization.'

What if my interest is not represented?

Nearly all of these groups were started by people who had an interest in the subject. Perhaps it is time to put something up on the company noticeboard.

Taking a sabbatical

Many companies offer sabbaticals to long-serving employees, allowing them to enjoy activities that full-time employment precludes. But what effect do they have on your career?

What constitutes a sabbatical?

It is time taken out of your career, often to pursue a personal goal and with the intention of returning to the same job; it can be paid or unpaid. There is no formal time allotment, but it is usually between three months and a year. 'A sabbatical needs to be long enough for you to really feel the difference and immerse yourself in whatever it is, but not so long that everything at your organization has changed,' says Julie Hurst, director of the Work Life Balance Centre.

Common pursuits include learning foreign languages, travelling, studying, writing a book or working on aid projects. 'Whatever you do, you should do something constructive,' says Rachel Morgan-Trimmer, founder of thecareerbreaksite.com. 'It doesn't have to be one thing [or another] either – many people combine.'

Why do it?

'If you've been at the same organization for a long time, a sabbatical can give you a certain freshness,' says executive coach Ros Taylor. 'It's great to get a view from somewhere else and take time out to think.'

Ms Hurst adds: 'Work often can't meet all people's psychological needs, which can leave you feeling a bit empty. Taking time out to address these can really get you up and running again.'

Sabbaticals are therefore taken more seriously than in the past. 'It used to be thought of as a bit of a jolly,' admits Ms Morgan-Trimmer. 'But it's now viewed as far more of a positive career step.'

Meanwhile, for employers they are an effective way to foster staff loyalty.

How do I prepare?

Ms Hurst says that a sabbatical should not be seen as a panacea. 'If you have problems at work, you need to address them rather than thinking that moving to a different environment will solve them for you. A sabbatical can help you rediscover the joy of work, but not by itself. You need to be moving towards a goal, not running away from something.'

You also need to plan properly. If you fail to do so, you may find yourself using your sabbatical to plan your sabbatical. Ms Morgan-Trimmer says preparation can be quite involved. 'If you've never worked in rural Africa before, you may not want to commit to it for three months, but you can now take two-week working mini breaks to see if it's for you.'

Ms Taylor says you need to plan going back to work, too: 'You shouldn't just dive in, it takes readjustment. Make sure you give yourself time to catch up.'

Finally, you should check what happens to your pension contributions.

What are the pitfalls?

Ms Taylor says that sometimes organizations do change very quickly. 'Even in a few months things could move on or you might miss out on a promotion,' notes Ms Taylor.

Ms Morgan-Trimmer says that you should also look at worst-case scenarios: 'You do need to think, "What if I hate it and come back in a month?" If your contract is very tightly worded and the sabbatical is unpaid, this can cause real problems.'

How to go on holiday

Your vacation might seem irrelevant to your career. However, not only are holidays a time to relax, recharge and reflect so that you return to work refreshed, but they are also exercises in delegation and empowerment. Yet many successful people find vacations so stressful that they would rather be in the office than on the beach.

How do I prepare?

For anything more than just a short break, start getting ready a month beforehand. 'You need to do as much as you can before you leave, but don't expect to be able to do everything – if you can, you're probably underemployed,' says Stella Brooks, co-founder of Inbucon, a London-based human resources consultancy. 'Clearing your holiday with your boss is the normal thing to do,' she adds, 'but really you should be clearing it with the person who sits next to you who has to pick up your work as well.'

What if I struggle with the idea of going on holiday at all?

You shouldn't. Many organizations formally encourage staff to take their full holiday allowance over the course of a year to prevent burnout. 'Your downtime for rest and relaxation makes you a better employee,' says Standolyn Robertson, a Boston-based personal organization expert.

Also, it's worth remembering that not taking statutory paid holiday is like taking a salary cut.

How long is it acceptable to be away?

Ms Brooks believes two weeks is more or less the limit, and more than three weeks makes things difficult – especially if you are more senior. 'If you're fairly junior, the office can usually live without you – and even in relatively senior positions, there will be someone who can stand in. You do hear of CEOs taking six weeks, although it's unusual,' she says.

How do I learn to stop worrying and love the beach?

Ideally, tie up as much as you can, delegate everything else and switch off. 'Some people can just do this, but others find it far harder,' says Brian Marien, director of Positive Health Strategies, a specialist health consultancy. 'The trouble is, at work, people learn to worry.' They ruminate on problems, which leads to further worry and anxiety, particularly if they feel they are not in control. 'People even worry about not worrying,' says Dr Marien.

As for the 'BlackBerry on the beach' problem, he concedes that cold turkey might be too much for some. 'Try to cut down – check it five times for the first day, then three times. By the second week, you might only need to check it once, if at all,' he says.

Ms Robertson advises not to bring a work mentality along to your vacation activities: 'Don't over-plan every minute of every day. There's nothing wrong with not seeing everything.'

What about emergencies?

Part of being a good manager is to give staff the tools and the opportunity to deal with day-to-day problems. They should not feel they need to contact you unless there really is a problem only you can solve.

As Ms Robertson says: 'Stay focused on your holiday. Work will be there when you get back.'

Being more enthusiastic

Everyone knows that enthusiasm boosts performance and that enjoying work can be the beginning of a virtuous circle. But can you become more enthusiastic?

How can I view my work more enthusiastically?

'Look at who ultimately benefits from the work you do,' says Octavius Black, founder of performance consultancy the Mind Gym. 'For instance, if you're an accountant, say, "I'm contributing to the trust that allows the business world to function." Make that link between what you do and the impact you have. It's incredibly powerful.'

Blaire Palmer, managing director of the coaching consultancy Taming Tigers, says people need to differentiate between motivation and inspiration in assessing their career. 'Motivation comes from outside, such as the need to earn money. But inspiration comes from finding meaning in your work,' she explains. 'You need to find your purpose and what really inspires you and remember that these things may well have changed since you started.'

Similarly, she says it is important to distinguish between what matters at work and what does not. 'People often think that every part of what they do is vitally important, but they should let go of some of the earnestness. Treat work like a marathon, not a sprint. That can make it more enjoyable.'

How much real control do I have?

'Unless you work on a production line, we all have scope to shape our job,' says Ceri Roderick, emeritus partner at business psychologists Pearn Kandola. 'People enjoy themselves much more when they're playing to their strengths so you need to ask what you are good at and how you can increase the amount of your working time you spend doing it.'

Mr Black says it is often small changes that make a big difference in how someone sees their job. 'Think about what you can do to make your job different in the future. Ask, "How can I set myself challenges or aim to be more of the person I want to be?" It can be as trivial as taking the stairs so you'll be fitter.'

In large organizations, altering a job can be comparatively easy. 'In a big company there'll be a niche for you, but you have to be proactive,' says Mr Roderick. 'People assume they'll be noticed, but you need to let those around know. Finally, look at your relationship with your boss, as this remains the single biggest reason people leave jobs.'

Ms Palmer suggests focusing on an individual task that you look forward to each day. 'It might be finishing a piece of work or lunch with a friend. Reconnect with people and don't spend all day on e-mail.'

What if I feel stuck?

'Sometimes it's OK to feel low,' says Mr Black. 'Give yourself a break. If you're getting nowhere, go and do something fun.'

Mr Roderick notes that just forcing yourself into action can help. 'There's a lot of inertia. Most people just don't get up and do it,' he says.

Ms Palmer says that just assessing the alternatives available can help. 'Know you have options. Know you're choosing your story.'

Chapter Seven
Being the bigger, better manager

How to manage former colleagues

You have just been promoted and are looking forward to your new role. The only trouble is, you are managing your old peers who, until now, were your equals. So how do you deal with your team now that you have become the boss that you used to moan about over a few drinks?

What should I expect?

'You won't have the same level of openness that you had with your peers,' says Miranda Kennett, an executive coach. For example, as soon as you step up, the quality of water cooler gossip you enjoy will go down.

Working relationships will also change upwards. 'The people who were previously your superiors will now be your peers,' says Ben Williams, Edinburgh-based corporate psychologist. 'You will need to form new relationships with them too.'

How should I behave?

'You mustn't let power go to your head,' says Owen Morgan, head of commercial operations at the consultancy Penna. 'Your behaviour towards your former peers should not change drastically – build on the existing trust and relationships you have.'

If you are unsure about something, there is nothing wrong with asking former colleagues with more experience for their input. You shouldn't do it all the time, but done occasionally it is flattering to them and humanizes you. Similarly, do not be afraid to ask for management training. Many people – especially in technical roles – can rise to quite a senior level on the back of their abilities, but have virtually no management experience.

What about my old friends?

There needs to be a demarcation line and you should set out people's roles and responsibilities (including your own) very clearly and play it absolutely straight, regardless of any previous allegiances. 'By being too chummy or showing favouritism, you won't impress your friends, but you will undermine your position as a manager,' says Ms Kennett.

As a manager, you may also find your views of previous colleagues changing. The best you can do is judge everyone on their performance and be scrupulously fair – and be seen to be scrupulously fair.

How do I deal with jealousy and resentment?

The egos of those who were not promoted may be bruised, although this can be ameliorated to some extent by good communication during the selection process. The best way to deal with this, however, is to show interest in the progression of those you now manage. 'Invest in people's careers,' says Mr Morgan. 'Talk to them about how they can advance.'

Mr Williams says one of the best things you can do to soothe any difficulties is to be pleasant: 'Develop a culture of praise around you. Make it a habit to praise people for good work – most bosses don't. Become someone everyone wants to do a good job for.'

Are there any good points?

Having worked on the ground with these people, you will have a good understanding of their skills, strengths and weaknesses, and motivations and concerns. This should make you a better and more realistic boss. In many ways, you are a far stronger person managing a team you know than taking over one you don't.

Being an effective interviewer

There is plenty of advice out there about how to succeed in interviews. Considerably less well covered is what to do when you are the interviewer. Yet the ability to recruit the right staff is one of the greatest challenges facing any manager – after all, you really will have to deal with the consequences.

How should I prepare?

'Make sure you've done your homework,' says Moira Benigson, managing partner of MBS Group, the executive search firm. 'Look over the job description, choose five to seven criteria to match candidates against and stick to these.'

How should I treat the candidate?

'Many people come across as very, very formal,' says Paul Falcone, vice-president for employee relations at Time Warner Cable and author of *96 Great Interview Questions to Ask Before You Hire.* 'Their philosophy is "The candidate has to get past me."' But, he explains, this is counterproductive: 'Make people feel comfortable with you and they'll open up.'

Jane Clarke, a director of business psychologists Nicholson McBride, adds that you should aim to leave a good impression yourself. 'Even if you don't offer them a job, you don't want them telling people what an awful experience they had.'

What should I look for?

Structuring interviews around competencies and behaviours is a popular approach. You should be looking for concrete evidence and plenty of solid examples. After that, you need to focus on compatibility. 'People often look for likeability,' says Mr Falcone. 'That is okay, but what is really important is being able to work together in terms of business style. You need to ask questions such as "How do you accept criticism and what are your time conventions?"'

With higher-level managers, he adds, he will often ask them to paint a picture of the kind of corporate culture they create. Finally, you need to understand a candidate's previous career progression. Falling remuneration and repetitive reasons for leaving previous jobs do not mean you should not employ the person, but they are flags. 'If I can understand how someone manages their career, then I can understand how they will manage in their job,' Mr Falcone says.

How should I structure my questions?

Avoid leading questions – people will just give you the answer they think you want. Also, try to stick to open-ended questions. 'They help to create a conversation,' says Ms Benigson. 'If you're a good interviewer, you should be chatting by the end.'

Ms Clarke gives this example: 'Instead of asking "Do you think integrity is important?" say "Can you give me examples of situations where integrity has featured?"'

What if I am still unsure?

'I sometimes ask candidates "What makes you stand out?"' Mr Falcone says. 'It's a great fall-back question if you're on the fence and can really change the direction of an interview. I've seen senior executives really struggle, but some people really enjoy the challenge. I once had a receptionist explain to me that she'd come up with an idea to save a $1 on every fax she sent. That's the kind of thing you're after.'

Sacking people

Sacking an employee can be one of the most difficult things any manager has to do. But it can also be highly necessary, reflect well on you and improve the work environment. And in some ways it is still a managerial rite of passage.

How do I prepare?

Make sure you know your organization's exit process, says Ian Gooden, chief operating officer of Chiumento, the human resources consultancy. 'A lot of people assume managers know how to do these things, but you can be a very established manager without ever having had to sack someone. If you're unsure, approach HR and ask for support.'

You may also want to speak to a mentor if you have one – this is exactly what they are there for.

Bear in mind that employment law differs from country to country. 'In the United States either party can terminate employment very easily at any time, though anti-discrimination law is much stronger than it is in the UK,' says Michael Burd, employment partner at the law firm Lewis Silkin. 'At the other end of the scale, in the Netherlands, you cannot dispense with someone's services without permission from a labour court.'

How should the process work?

'It should be a series of logical steps, rather than something that comes as a bolt out of the blue,' says Mr Gooden. 'If it comes as a shock to the employee, your communication probably hasn't been very good.'

There need to be meetings, discussions, opportunities for the person to put their case and, where appropriate, help and support. 'When it's managed properly, many people will jump before they're pushed,' says Mr Gooden. 'They're savvy enough to know that it's better to be able to say, "I left for these reasons" than "I left because I was sacked."'

What about the actual termination?

Even in your final meeting, the employee should be given a chance to say their piece. Ideally as a manager you should have an idea of how the individual will respond. But people are unpredictable and reactions can run the whole gamut from extreme emotional outburst to relief.

If things do get heated, Charles Woodruffe, managing director at Human Assets, the business psychologists, says it is important not to get emotionally dragged in. 'Keep the conversation objective and factual; stay calm and focused. Be as humane as possible but don't blur the message. If you're going to agonize, do it in private, not when you're sacking the person. You want to be empathetic, but not too empathetic, and avoid using terrible clichés.'

What about those who remain behind?

'You'll often find that the person's team were very frustrated with their poor performance, so doing something about it can make you look decisive,' says Mr Woodruffe – just so long as they believe the process was fair and just.

Similarly, those above you are likely to see it as proof that you can step up to the mark and deal with unpleasant situations.

However, it can be problematic for you. 'The manager who dismissed the person can feel guilty for months afterwards,' says Mr Gooden, 'although if it's been done properly, you shouldn't.'

In the end, you must tell yourself that it is a business decision and not personal.

'It's a nasty thing you've had to do,' says Mr Woodruffe, 'but that's what you're paid for.'

Delegating effectively

Climbing the corporate ladder requires you to hand over day-to-day tasks to others. But many people find this very difficult to do – or do it in a way that leaves everyone feeling unhappy and demotivated.

What are the most common problems?

'Dodgy delegators fall into two camps,' says Geraldine Gallacher of the Executive Coaching consultancy. 'The "no-one-does-it-as-well-as-I-can" brigade and the abdicators who hand over a task and forget to follow up unless there's a problem. Or, put more crudely, the former are control freaks and the latter are lazy. The less healthy economy of recent years has also seen a rise in micromanagement, in areas such as expenses.'

How do you overcome a fear of letting go?

'Once people experiment with delegating and find that disasters don't happen they get more confident and do more of it and it can be a virtuous circle,' says Ms Gallacher.

This process does not necessarily need to stem from work. She notes that women returning to work after having children often seem to have developed abilities in this area as 'there is no greater test of your appetite for delegation than handing your baby over to someone else'.

Octavius Black, founder of the Mind Gym, suggests trying to imagine the alternative: 'If it helps, think about yourself in the future – do you really want to be doing the same stuff that you've been doing for the last five years?'

How do I delegate well?

You need to put in the upfront investment to get the return. Those to whom you are going to cede control need to be carefully selected and properly briefed.

'Agree the path for the task together then decide when and how you'll review against progress and define what is good and what will cause problems,' Mr Black says.

This may seem a lot of hassle in the short term, but it is an investment in the medium term.

'Create a sense of ownership and empowerment,' adds Virginia Merritt, managing partner of organizational consultancy Stanton Marris. 'The phrase we use is "freedom within a framework". But don't let go fully as that can be very demotivating. Monitor, but don't meddle; follow up and offer support.'

What should I delegate?

'The question you always need to ask here is: "Can this task or decision be done or made by someone below me?" If they have the knowledge or capability, then do it,' says Ms Merritt. 'Hang on to broad horizon things.'

Mr Black says you should keep the areas where you can really make a real difference. 'Recruitment is one, as who you employ is so important. It's generally things about people and you can't really delegate important relationships. Great CEOs usually manage people and not an enormous amount else.'

Who gets the credit?

If members of your team do well, make sure they get the credit. This is a great motivator for them and reflects very well on you as a leader – but if you take the credit for others' hard work the reverse will be true. Do not be insecure about this: those above you are likely to see a manager who draws attention to their troops' achievements as confident and mature.

Personal outsourcing

In our work and domestic lives, we all have low-value tasks that sap our productivity. But how do you outsource them to focus on the things that matter?

What should I target?

'One person's hassle is another's necessity,' says Jim Maxmin, author of *The Support Economy*. 'Keep a diary and look for the things you don't enjoy.'

Clare Evans, a time management coach, says: 'Know the value of your time. Especially if you charge by the hour, you should ask if certain tasks represent the most value you can add. If you're charging £250 an hour, it makes total sense to pay a PA to deal with tasks like e-mail and letters if they charge £15 an hour. Important and higher-value tasks may also be worth delegating if they're things you're not good at.'

Alex Cheatle, founder of the lifestyle management company Ten, says you should use support to break the back of big administrative tasks. 'For example, a lot of people still use paper address books because transferring the whole thing over is such a pain and they're always too busy. Paying someone to spend four hours doing this can be very helpful,' he says.

As for personal tasks at home, he adds, you should think beyond hiring gardeners and cleaners. 'Given the overlap between work and life, 24/7 support of some sort can help. One of our busiest times is Sunday evening when people prepare for the week ahead.'

How do I outsource these tasks properly?

Ms Evans says that taking the time to show people how to do things well is a wise investment. 'Explain it properly and then you won't have to do it again ... Ask yourself how you can document processes.'

You should also pass tasks on at the right time. 'Rather than getting halfway through solving something yourself, write a brief and give it to an expert – don't delegate too late,' says Mr Cheatle. He also stresses the importance of finding the right people. 'It might be wrong to delegate complex travel itineraries to a PA who will be using Expedia.'

He adds that you need to provide the means to carry out your tasks, such as credit cards. 'A lot of people expect their PAs to be able to sort things out and then give them none of the tools to do so.'

How can I use technology?

There are many high-tech ways to streamline your life – from online shopping to virtual assistants that work from their own homes. Mr Cheatle suggests finding a helpful geek. 'People over 35 tend to get left behind with new technology. Find a bright young thing and say: "Here is my life. What five apps should I be using?" A [taxi company] app can save you from doing wasteful things like calling your PA to book a car.'

What should I not outsource?

Ms Evans advises to be careful about delegating confidential work unless the person you are giving it to is trusted. Moreover, she adds: 'You shouldn't dump tasks on people just because you don't want to do them, as this can look very bad.'

Finally, you should try not to outsource things that you actually enjoy doing – no matter how trivial they might seem.

Managing an under-performer

Under-performing underlings represent a huge challenge for any manager. Not only are they very difficult, but their poor performance can rub off on you.

What do I look out for?

'The first thing to do is to trust your instincts as a boss,' says Virginia Merritt, a partner at strategy consultants Stanton Marris. 'You notice very early on when someone isn't performing at their best. But it is very easy to rationalize, make excuses and hope that by ignoring a problem it will go away.' However, she adds: 'You need to call it out as soon as you know it's happening and sound a warning bell that it's not acceptable.'

How do I understand the under-performance?

'There's a big difference between under-performers who always underperform and those who have only just started underperforming,' says Octavius Black, founder of performance consultancy the Mind Gym. 'If they have performed well in the past you need to ask: "What's wrong now?" Find the issue and ring-fence it.'

Alan Redman, a director at business psychologists Criterion Partnership, says: 'Try to understand the causes of the underperformance. They might be things outside work, they might be personality based, the person might be overwhelmed by the job or it could be their motivation or values.'

How do I turn it round?

'Engage with the person,' says Mr Redman. 'Be open, honest and frank. Build on their strengths and stress the positives. Try and have solution-focused discussions. Ask questions in a way that forces the person to accept that change can happen.'

Mr Black says that they may not be able to see the upsides. 'Give them a carrot. Maybe they can't see the benefit of what they bring. Explore it with them. There's every reason to believe the situation can be turned around.'

If somebody is a constant under-performer, he says, you may need to show what good performance looks like, as they might not know. 'Break it down for them. Give them granular goals. Agree what success looks like.'

How do I ensure the turnround continues?

'Don't just agree performance goals verbally; write them down for people and say we'll review these in X months,' says Ms Merritt. 'Tell the individual you need to hear about the improvement from other people too. They need to realize colleagues notice and judge.'

However, Mr Redman adds: 'Be honest with yourself. Some people cannot make a success of the role they're in.'

How do I ensure poor performance doesn't rub off on me?

'I'd go to my own manager and say: "This is a problem I have." Ask them for advice,' says Mr Black. 'That way they know and they feel good because you're asking them for help.'

He adds that poor performance must be dealt with. 'The mistake many people make is, they don't have those tough conversations. If you let people be a bit crap, it's contagious. You get social loafing. If one person underperforms, other people often do too.'

Being a mentor

From management consultancies to TV talent shows, everyone seems to agree that having a mentor is an excellent idea. But how do you actually mentor someone? And is there more to it than just the odd pep talk and an occasional state-of-their-career chat over a drink?

What does mentoring involve?

Frances Cook, a director at Penna, the human resources consultancy, defines mentoring as 'the informal transmission of knowledge and social capital along with psychological support'. In practice, this means giving someone the benefit of your experience across all areas of professional and personal life.

Steven Varlakhov, a vice-president at Deutsche Bank who hosts a mentoring circle, explains: 'When you're new to an organization and industry you can be overwhelmed. You might not be able to talk to parents and friends as they may not understand what you're going through. It's giving our junior bankers someone who understands the challenges they face that they can talk to, whether it's promotion, career development or personal issues.'

While mentors and mentees might have regular, scheduled meetings, ideally the mentor should be there whenever they are needed. And, of course, the relationship must be completely confidential.

Is it just for new recruits?

Being mentored can be invaluable for younger employees. 'You feel very privileged to get one-to-one time with a real high flyer,' explains Alice Cooper, a mentee who recently qualified as an accountant at PwC, the professional services firm.

But Ms Cook points out that even the top brass of a company can benefit from talking to someone 'who's been there and done it and can provide real advice and support'. For example, she says that, at board level, you can work through 'difficult areas like conflict, divided boards or credibility issues'.

What qualities does a mentor need?

'You sometimes help people deal with areas like spouses and family issues which can affect work so you need a sensitive approach,' says Mr Varlakhov.

'People share a lot of information with you, so you need to be happy with that and really like people,' says Sandra Rodger, a director at PwC. 'In a previous company someone asked me if I had five minutes. I was very busy, but the person really looked like they needed five minutes so I stopped to talk to them. They were about to hand in their resignation and probably would have left if I hadn't spoken to them.'

What does the mentor get out of it?

'It gives you a chance to understand what juniors have on their minds and to build relationships,' says Mr Varlakhov.

'For some people, being a mentor can be a new phase of their working life. It quite often gives real satisfaction late in careers,' adds Ms Cook.

Ms Rodger adds: 'When someone you've mentored does well you feel fantastic.' She also points out you can build up valuable networks if your former mentees leave for other companies.

How to stay engaged with your job

Managers are encouraged to keep staff engaged. But how do they stay engaged themselves? And can you turn round a job that has become boring to you?

Is my glass half full?

'If you're happy, you're automatically engaged, so start by thinking about what makes you happy in what you do,' says Jessica Pryce-Jones, chief executive of iOpener, a workplace happiness consultancy.

Octavius Black, founder of performance consultancy the Mind Gym, says part of the challenge in staying enthused is that work is where few people expect to find happiness: 'However, studies show that many people are likelier to find happiness at work than not. You need to recognize what work provides and the needs it meets – it offers friendships, conversation and challenges.'

How do I boost my sense of engagement?

An awareness of being part of something big is helpful, says Ms Pryce-Jones. But she adds: 'A lot of what motivates you on a day-to-day basis is actually quite small.' Look for meaning in what you do: 'It affects everyone from CEOs to janitors. You need to think about how you make a difference – who benefits from what you do?'

Mr Black says long-term personal objectives help: 'Set yourself challenging goals. Just doing this may force you to reshape your role.'

Is there anything I can do outside my current role?

Charles Woodruffe, managing director of business psychologists Human Assets, says: 'First ask [yourself] if you can expand your role or add to your professional development. Or you could look for engagement elsewhere in the company. Many organizations take social responsibility very seriously.'

Ms Pryce-Jones says improving engagement could even come from activities outside the workplace that feed back into your job: 'If you look at the volunteers who work on Linux, they put in enormous amounts of unpaid work and are very engaged in what they're doing.'

Are there simple ways to jog myself out of a rut?

'Do something, no matter how small,' says Ms Pryce-Jones. 'One of the most important things for mental and physical well-being is a perception of control. It could be as simple as talking to someone you've never talked to before. You can also work on your confidence – as confidence is the precursor to action.'

Talk things over with others, says Mr Woodruffe, but: 'If you're in a group that's stuck in a rut, don't join in with the grumbling groupthink.'

Should I cut my losses?

'You need to ask if you can reframe your work as interesting and stimulating,' says Mr Black. 'Are there obstacles you can remove? Work out what it is you dislike and if you can, change it. If you can't, there's no point and you need to move on.'

Or, as Mr Woodruffe puts it: 'Don't try to put a sticking plaster on a serious disease.'

How to motivate your staff

Highly motivated staff perform well, enjoy their jobs, go the extra mile for you and stick around. But what actually gets them out of bed in the morning?

How important is money?

It is often said that money is not a huge tool to engage staff, but this is only half the story. 'You have to pay people enough money,' says Daniel Pink, the Washington-based author of *Drive: The Surprising Truth About What Motivates Us*. 'If you don't, it is a demotivator. But once you pay them enough – the market rate or slightly above – each extra unit of pay has very little effect.'

As for bonuses, Phil Merrell, a director at the human resources consultancy Penna, says they tend to have a 'short-term euphoric effect' but do not have a huge impact on overall engagement – particularly when they become the norm.

What really motivates people?

Mr Merrell says a key is to let people get on with their jobs. 'Good managers give people compasses, not maps. Give them a level of discretion and they'll make discretionary effort for you.'

You need to listen to people as well. Make sure that they feel their opinions count and that they are valued. A feeling of belonging and purpose also motivates. 'It's a sense of making progress and being part of something bigger than yourself,' Mr Pink says. 'People should feel like they're making a contribution to something important.'

A good illustration of this is the (probably apocryphal) story of the janitor at Nasa who was asked by President John F Kennedy what he did. The janitor replied: 'I'm helping to put a man on the moon.'

Staff should also feel their own careers are progressing, says Richard Phelps, a partner at PwC, the professional services firm. 'Focus on the development needs of individuals. People want to further their careers – you need to show them there's a future for them.'

How does motivation differ by job?

So-called 'if–then' motivators (for example, if you pack a thousand boxes of eggs, then you receive a £50 bonus) work well for assembly-line work, as they focus the mind. But, according to Mr Pink, they are of limited value elsewhere. 'For creative, conceptual and complex work – in other words, most white-collar work – you don't want that narrow, controlling focus, so using "if–then" motivators can backfire.'

Better, he says, are schemes such as the one at Google that allows staff to spend 20 per cent of their time pursuing projects that interest them. Freeing people up to do things their way is hugely motivating. But companies find this difficult. 'A lot of mechanisms inside organizations are about ensuring compliance. You don't want compliance: you want to free people up to become engaged in their own way,' he says.

What about my role as a manager?

It is worth remembering that the number one reason people cite for leaving jobs is their boss. As well as being flexible and understanding, Mr Phelps says you should take a genuine interest in staff: 'As a boss, you've got to give some of yourself back.'

Building a team

Teams form the basis of virtually every organization. So how do you go about building a good one and what do you need to watch for?

What do you want to achieve?

'Start by asking what the purpose of the team is,' says David Pendleton, a founder of Edgecumbe, the organizational psychologists. 'You want to build a team to do something significant and align them to that purpose.'

Jon Katzenbach, author of *The Wisdom of Teams*, agrees: 'You don't want to go to the effort of forming a team if you don't have a team task.'

How do I get the right mix?

Executive coach Miranda Kennett says most of us tend to be quite good at picking individuals for specific skills, but there are other things to consider. 'While you should recruit for function, you need to be aware of informal roles too. Some people are very good social cement while others are pioneers. It's personalities as well as skills.'

You should also avoid clones, recruiting in your own image and selecting only the best and the brightest – a team full of brilliant visionaries will have nobody to do the dull detail work.

What about leadership?

Mr Katzenbach says it is important to differentiate between two types of team: the single leadership unit, which is a team with one leader; and a real team where there is no fixed leader.

Single leadership units, he explains, can be very fast and efficient, but real teams tend to be more flexible, resilient and accountable – and have greater peer respect.

'One of the best places to find real teams is in elite military units. If you look at teams in the US Marine Corps, every member is trained to lead, because every member may have to be a leader.'

Mr Katzenbach says there are a lot of gradations along the spectrum, such as leaders who only step up when needed.

What if I'm adding to or merging existing teams?

'If you're bringing two teams together, assess people individually,' says Mr Pendleton. 'Watch out for overlap or redundancy of roles. Gaps can be better than duplication as teams where everyone is competing to make the same contribution become very Darwinian; sometimes you will need to get rid of people.'

Ms Kennett says: 'Like any social group, new people have a need to be acknowledged, accepted and appreciated. Each new person changes the team dynamic subtly and other members need to flex a bit. New members should spend time with individual team members to form proper relationships.'

How do I get them to work together?

'The biggest problem with teamwork is ego,' says Mr Pendleton. 'Some of the best teamworkers I know have their egos under control.'

Ms Kennett says you need to go through the steps of team formation: forming, storming, 'norming' and performing. 'Successful teams are coherent and cohesive. The individuals may not even like each other, but they have found a way of working together effectively.'

Managing your way through a merger

Working for a company that is merging with another or being taken over can be an unsettling experience full of imposed change. But it can also present great career opportunities.

How do I approach the situation?

'It's a transition and you have to plan for it,' says business psychologist Gary Fitzgibbon. 'You're likely to have a lot of concerns about your status and position prior to the merger. You need to make these explicit and find out as much as possible about what's happening; be clear in your own mind about what your concerns are.'

Peter Shaw, an executive coach at Praesta, says: 'Be honest and objective about the implications for you. Recognize that there's an emotional process you go through and that you may experience anger, gloom and even grief. But you must accept the new reality – you can't rail against the wind.'

Sometimes, he says, a symbolic act such as cutting up your old business cards can help.

How do I make the best of the situation?

Mr Fitzgibbon says that although you are unlikely to be able to affect the course of events, simply taking action and keeping informed is often enough to overcome feelings of helplessness and reduce anxiety.

'Stress is often to do with the combined effect of many small annoying changes,' he says. 'Often they're things that can be rectified but instead, you let them become overwhelming and they ferment. If you know in advance that something is going to affect you, you can start preparing to accommodate it.'

Mr Shaw says you should look for the good in the situation: 'Ask yourself "What does this open up? Will there be more jobs or opportunities to get wider experience?" For example, if you're a domestic company being bought by an international organization there may be opportunities abroad.'

Scott Moeller, a professor at Cass Business School and author of *Intelligent M&A: Navigating the Mergers and Acquisitions Minefield*, advises that you do not depend on anyone else. 'Take everyone's advice with a pinch of salt,' he says, 'especially those higher up as they are more likely to be made redundant. Also remember power bases can change very quickly.'

What can I do to safeguard my position?

'For someone relatively junior, the main thing to do is to be on committees or teams that are looking to deal with the integration,' says Professor Moeller. 'It is not a time to be quiet. Those who are extroverted and play political games tend to come out on top. This is the time to pull out all the stops and not the time to go on holiday.'

You also need a plan B: particularly if you are senior, now is the time to be talking to headhunters and tapping your contacts.

What if I'm in the line of fire?

Remain calm. 'Of course, some jobs will be at risk but you must not let it become a self-fulfilling prophecy,' says Mr Shaw. 'Stay positive and don't get on a downward spiral.'

Professor Moeller adds that there are upsides too – especially if you are looking for a change anyway. 'Redundancy packages during M&A are often considerably better because you're part of a large group,' he says.

Running an away day

Done right, an away day can be an opportunity to plan strategy, deal with a variety of issues and build esprit de corps; done wrong it can be a waste of an expensive hotel.

How do you make an away day pay?

'You need to have clear objectives,' says Paul Kearns, a consultant on strategic corporate events. 'Communicate what it is you're trying to achieve beforehand. If you don't have objectives you often won't produce anything.'

You should also ensure the right people attend. 'If it is a serious meeting, you need the key players there,' says Mr Kearns. 'Important people can sometimes show contempt for these things.'

How do I run the day?

'You need to recognize the ebb and flow of people's biorhythms,' says Phil Anderson, client director at Ashridge Business School. 'Don't have a PowerPoint presentation when people are feeling sleepy just after lunch. Spice it up and, if you are leading, get others to lead certain parts as people get bored with the same speaker.

'You need to think about breaks too; you often get insights over coffee when talking less formally.'

The ideal day should combine serious business with fun and relaxation. 'Games can work but they need to be appropriate to the organization,' says Mr Anderson. 'Even with a strict business focus, it's good to get people to do something different.'

As away days tend to generate a lot of ideas, you should also evaluate as you go, so you don't end up with hundreds of flip charts at the end of the session.

What if there are disagreements?

Simmering resentments often boil over at such events. 'Anticipate that there may be tensions,' says Jane Clarke of business psychologists Nicholson McBride. 'You might get an HR person to do a bit of research – what are the personality issues?'

If there are tensions, it's good to air them at the start, rather than letting them come out in the bar. 'The rules of engagement need to be spelt out – and the difference between constructive and destructive criticism explained – or it can become a general bitching session,' warns Mr Kearns.

If things are difficult, it can make sense to have a professional facilitator.

How long should it be?

'Overnights are good,' says Ms Clarke. 'A lot of talking takes place in the bar or over dinner and you get a chance to work on both business strategy and individual relationships.'

Mr Anderson points out that you should also remember that people have other commitments. 'Don't make it too long. Arriving the night before and then finishing in the afternoon is good.'

What about follow up?

'A lot of people leave feeling very motivated and then nothing happens,' says Ms Clarke. This is often because the organizer attempts to do everything themselves afterwards.

'A good way to ensure follow up happens is to give everyone something to do,' says Mr Anderson. 'That should happen before you leave. You also need to agree a follow-up date to check which next steps have been taken and by whom.'

Managing clever but lazy employees

The German general Kurt von Hammerstein-Equord is noted for saying that clever, lazy people were qualified for the highest leadership duties. But how do you manage staff who don't need to try?

Ask yourself if they're actually lazy

'It could be that their personal style is more laid back – they may appear lazy without actually being so,' says Willma Tucker, a consultant at talent and career specialists Right Management. 'In this case, you may need to tackle the perception that they do less, especially if others think this is the case.'

Peter Taylor, author of *The Lazy Project Manager*, says, 'The big thing is, are people contributing? If they're doing their fair share, I'd hope others would ask how they do it.'

You should also examine your own motivations. Some managers feel threatened by the ablest members of their team and treat them unfairly as a result.

How do I deal with them if they really are doing very little?

'Focus on the positives rather than the negatives,' says Mr Taylor. 'Being lazy in a traditional sense is probably as hard work as being productive. Try and explain this and turn their thinking round.'

Jane Barrett, a career coach and co-author of *If Not Now When? How to Take Charge of Your Career*, says: 'The key thing here is motivation. You often hear of very bright people never achieving much as they lack motivation. You need to uncover their strengths and preferences. Find out what their skills, interests and values are. Look at the kind of environment they work best in.'

Ms Tucker adds, 'It's often about enjoyment. Sometimes talented individuals just aren't that engaged. They may not fully understand their contributions or feel their manager respects and values them.'

What if they are just not delivering to their high potential?

This is tougher as you have no real basis for complaint. Mr Taylor says: 'In an ideal situation, you'd put people who are dragging a bit with the stars of the team. You should attempt to inspire them … Ask them what they want to do and focus on the places where they can really deliver.'

However, you need to be careful. 'There's nothing really wrong with someone putting in an 80-hour week and someone putting in a 30-hour week if they're both delivering the same level of results,' says Mr Taylor. 'You should also remember work–life balance. You might see someone as a bit lazy, but their priority may not be becoming a CEO.'

If they start to perform, won't they just move on?

Talented people are the biggest differentiator in most businesses today and if you can develop and promote them it reflects well on you. 'They do move on very quickly and that will make you look good,' says Ms Tucker. 'Don't see them as a threat and don't hold them back. They'll go anyway. It is better that they go with your blessing.'

How to lead a U-turn

Being able to bring people along with you is an important leadership quality. But how do you convince them to stay with you if you have to change direction?

How do I plan for a U-turn?

First, ask yourself if you're really making a U-turn. 'Sometimes what might initially appear to be a U-turn can be presented as a reaction to new information or circumstances,' says Peter Shaw, an executive coach at Praesta. 'Your opponents may want to describe it as a U-turn, but that doesn't mean you should.'

Second, make sure that you're very unlikely to have to change direction again – everyone is allowed one U-turn, but serial volte-faces rightly lead to charges of flip-flopping.

How do I present it?

Politics has done business a disservice in this respect, says Virginia Merritt, a partner at strategy consultants Stanton Marris. 'The political view is typified by Margaret Thatcher's line "This lady is not for turning," and suggests that making a U-turn is a sign of weakness. But in business it's often the opposite. There can be more strength in showing you are human and you do get it wrong – as long as you're upfront in showing why you changed.'

To this end, you need to set out your thinking clearly and concisely and offer objective evidence and data to support your case. You should keep your message consistent; Mr Shaw notes that the initial reaction of many people to a U-turn is: 'Are we getting the whole story?' which is why consistency of message is key.

You might also explain that your change of direction shows that you're open to new points of view and that you listen to people. Mr Shaw adds that it's not just what you say, but also how you say it: 'People can see how you react. If you look humiliated you will lose credibility.'

What should I expect the reaction to be?

Your change of direction might be pragmatic but your team may struggle with it, says Justin Spray, a director of business psychologists Mendas. 'A lot can be explained by cognitive dissonance – the discomfort we feel when we try to reconcile conflicting views, beliefs and ideas. Although the reaction might not appear rational, it is quite common for people to show feelings such as anger, guilt and embarrassment.'

He notes that you will have turned part of your team's world view upside-down and they may well initially conclude that you are a less capable leader so that they don't feel so bad about themselves.

How can I deal with this?

'Recognize and don't belittle their emotional reaction,' says Mr Spray. 'It might seem irrational and ridiculous to you but it is a predictable human reaction. Allow them to work through the emotions and work hard to find the commonly held view or value that still underpins the new approach.'

Mr Shaw notes that a further problem with U-turns is that people may feel their efforts have been wasted. 'Make sure you thank people for the contribution they've made even if it now turns out they were made in the wrong direction. Otherwise they can become demoralized and their engagement can suffer.'

Chapter Eight
Goals, career planning, business education and other longer-term stuff

How to set career goals

Every now and then – and particularly at certain milestones – it's good to take a little time out to think about what our career goals are and how we're going to reach them. But what are the best ways to set goals? And how do you ensure you'll stick to them?

How do I plan my goals?

Richard Brown, managing partner at Cognosis, a London-based strategy consultancy, says: 'You should have three goals or less. Any more and you won't be able to focus on them.'

When considering your goals for the next, say, 12 months, think about how they fit into where you are heading over the next five years. 'It may help to see them in the light of your longer-term vision for your career,' says Mr Brown.

How do I make sure my goals are right for me?

'The two main factors are your personality and the nature of the goal,' says Jane Clarke, a director at business psychologists Nicholson

McBride. 'Where we go wrong is that we assume that what works for one successful person will work for you. But you will often find on some level that you don't want it enough. So you need to think about your motivation – for instance, is it status or work–life balance? Look back over your career – what has worked?'

Ms Clarke also suggests using the technique of 'reframing', which involves trying to view goals that may not initially feel very 'you' in terms of the benefits they can bring you. You could also visualize how you will feel when you have achieved your goals.

My goals look like mountains. Where do I start?

'Break them down,' says Standolyn Robertson, a personal organization expert. 'If any part seems overwhelming, then you have not broken it down enough. Individual tasks have to be within reach.' For instance, if your goal is to change career, step one is rewriting your CV.

Ms Robertson also advises getting organized, by which she does not mean tidying your desk (although that may help); rather, you need to deal with the problems that are preventing you focusing on career goals.

How do I make sure I stay on track?

If you are serious about attaining goals, you should prioritize them over everything else, says Ms Clarke. Just as important, you should make sure that those around you understand your priorities. This goes for everything from 'I'm going to raise my profile' to 'I'm going to pick my kids up from school twice a week.'

This does not mean you should not do ordinary, day-to-day work; but it does mean that working towards the goal should not constantly take a back seat to ordinary work. Learn to distinguish between what is urgent and what is important. So, block off time in your diary to achieve your goal and treat it as you would any other business engagement.

You should also keep track of your progress. Give yourself deadlines and appraise yourself monthly or quarterly.

'You should keep your goals close to hand,' says Mr Brown. 'Have them on cards on your desk or on a screen saver.'

It is a good idea to share the goal with someone else at work. Two people are far more likely to stick with something than one. Alternatively, you could turn to a coach. 'Anything that gives you accountability will help you achieve your goals,' says Ms Robertson.

Future proofing your career

In today's uncertain economy just keeping your job can feel like a full-time occupation. But rather than firefighting, you should take a strategic view of your long-term employability, ensuring you have the skills current and future employers want.

Where do I start?

'Get used to the idea that what you know has a shorter and shorter lifespan,' says Ian Pearson, a futurologist at the consultancy Futurizon. 'You need to be learning continuously.' Mr Pearson recommends a 'blurred focus' for this: 'Spend 15 per cent of your time learning about fields adjacent to yours. It's a bit like the ecology of a rainforest – you don't want to be the animal who is so fantastically well adapted to one tree that they will die if that tree is cut down.' Miranda Kennett, founder of First Class Coach, recommends regular checks to ensure that you're constantly adding employability and experience: 'Rewrite your CV every year. If you can't find something new to add to it then look at yourself.' She notes that even when times are tough, companies usually still offer some training.

How can I make my relationships and networks help?

People tend to spend less time on working relationships as workloads have increased due to cuts, says Stephen Viscusi, author of

Bulletproof Your Job. This, he believes, is a mistake as there are probably plenty of people who can do your job, but rather fewer who are liked and trusted. The most important working relationship is with your boss. 'If you make your boss happy, they will keep you on,' Mr Viscusi says.

What about my sector?

Think carefully about where you work. 'There are sectors which change less and sectors which are more resilient to change,' says Mr Pearson. 'You should be picking organizations which are already future proofed. If you are working in the auto industry, moving into electric cars might be a good idea as that's likely to be a growth area.' Mr Viscusi adds that, in the near future, one should have realistic salary expectations: 'There's a new frugality about. Recognizing this will make you psychologically more employable.' In fact, being slightly underpaid may be no bad thing at the moment as it makes you less visible to cost-cutters.

Can my state of mind help?

'You need to be agile and adaptable,' says Mr Pearson. 'People get very loyal to companies and very upset when they collapse or shed jobs.' It is important to be resilient. 'You need to be someone who lands on their feet and who is psychologically ready to move,' Mr Pearson adds. Mr Viscusi says that companies (and bosses) want can-do people who make their lives easier. 'At the moment a lot of people who've come through the recession are in a real funk – they're like damaged goods. Don't moan about how bad it's been. Focus on the positives and be optimistic.' It may be obvious but one of the best ways of ensuring positivity is to have a job you like.

Should I plan for emergencies?

Of course, the easiest time to find a new job is when you already have one. But, says Ms Kennett, 'Always have a plan B for if things go horribly wrong.'

Should I do an MBA?

If the job market is tough, instead of struggling through, it can make sense to take time out and add to your CV. Equally, even if you're highly employable, an MBA can be a way of enhancing your employability and boosting your earning power. Regardless of your reasons for doing it, how do you make the most of it?

How do I fully exploit the experience?

Alongside the boost in earnings it offers, the increased employability and the new career channels it opens, an MBA also provides some stealthier benefits for those prepared to work them. There will be few other times when you enjoy such sustained exposure to future movers and shakers.

Most schools have active alumni associations to help you make the most of the contacts you establish. 'The alumni network is like a giant little black book you can access years after you leave,' says Jenny Soderlind, alumni communications manager at London Business School.

How do I minimize the cost?

MBAs are not cheap: Harvard puts the cost of tuition and board for one year at over $75,000. You need to add the salary you will be forgoing while you study. It is important to recognize that if you are going to be a student again, you will, to some extent, have to live like a student.

However, there are ways to lessen the financial burden. Some employers offer assistance for career development. Bursaries and scholarships are available from many schools and are always worth investigating – especially if you come from an atypical MBA background. Various government loans may also be available.

An MBA is also a huge investment of time. Many people who do them are married with children so you will need to explain to your four-year-old why you need to study on Saturdays.

Is an MBA always useful?

In some sectors, an MBA is virtually a prerequisite, but in others it might be viewed as a positively eccentric career choice.

'Like all degrees, MBAs are becoming more common and less of a differentiator than they were, especially from lower-ranked schools,' says career coach Corinne Mills of Personal Career Management.

However, she notes, there are areas where the reverse is still true. 'If you worked in the voluntary sector or some areas of the public sector, I'd expect that an MBA really would be valuable and would make you stand out.'

An MBA also confers bragging rights. Like most higher degrees it is perfectly acceptable to put 'MBA' after your name on a business card, whereas alluding to your undergraduate degree tends to make you look slightly ridiculous. So, if you want to tell people you went to Harvard, this is the socially acceptable way to do so. In a similar way, an MBA can also help compensate for a lacklustre undergraduate degree.

What is the case against?

Some argue that the financial case may not stack up as it once did. Gabriel Hammond, a partner at Alerian Capital Management, says that he did not do an MBA while at Goldman Sachs, where traditionally it would have been an obvious step, because the price in terms of forgone salary would have been so high and because he believed that 'a lot of what is taught in the classroom can be learned on the job'. However, he does add that this may only be true of the portfolio management side of finance.

Getting your employer to support your MBA

Given the financially onerous cost of MBAs, many people try to get their employers to pick up part or all of the tab. But how do you persuade them to do this, while also convincing them you won't use your new qualification to jump ship?

What forms can support take?

'Financial support is one element,' says Virginie Fougea, senior manager at INSEAD's admissions office. 'This could mean you're paid while you're away or you could be sponsored. But support can also mean letting you take a sabbatical or unpaid leave.'

How do I convince my company they will get a return on their investment?

'You need to explain that they will get someone who is more able to contribute to the organization's objectives,' says Ms Fougea. 'They will gain someone who can think and act quickly and objectively and who is groomed to think strategically. They will also benefit from someone who has a very strong network of contacts and can leverage it.'

What about loyalty?

'It's a two-way deal between you and your company,' says Eric Cornuel, director-general of the European Foundation for Management Development. 'Helping people to do MBAs is a way of developing an environment where talent is retained and developed.'

He adds that perhaps people are looking at it the wrong way: rather than trying to convince a company that you will not leave, you should explain that an MBA is more likely to make you stay. 'You can't ask managers to be loyal to companies if companies are not loyal to managers ... Investing in people's future is a part of a social and economic contract.'

Dave Wilson, president and chief executive of the Graduate Management Admission Council, points out that if you invest in someone's future, they tend to believe they have one. 'By and large any candidate who gets their MBA paid for is likely to be more loyal, not less,' he says.

Are there more concrete ways of ensuring loyalty?

Mr Wilson says that one scheme that works well is that the candidate takes out a loan in their name, which the company pays off over three years; that way, if they leave, the loan is theirs. People also sometimes sign contracts stating that they will remain for some period after their MBA or have to pay back some of the cost.

You could also offer to share the knowledge you gain with others in the company, either during the course or on your return.

Does it make a difference if I do it part time?

Mr Wilson says recruiters tend to focus on the full timers. 'You see two groups of people doing MBAs – career changers and career accelerators,' he explains. 'Changers tend to do them full time and want to swap roles, from, say, engineering to banking. Accelerators are trying to move their career on from wherever they might be and are much more likely to do part-time MBAs.'

Is there a payback time?

It is a good idea for both sides to have a rough understanding of when you might reasonably be considered to have paid your debt to the company so that you can do whatever you want with a clear conscience. 'Typically, I think it's between two and five years although it varies with sector,' says Ms Fougea.

Alternatives to MBAs

MBAs may be the obvious choice when it comes to business education, but given their cost in terms of time, fees and forgone salary, it can sometimes be worth exploring other options.

Why should I consider the alternatives to an MBA?

'MBAs are really good ways for individuals to improve their general management capabilities,' says Michael Stanford, executive director of Partnership Programmes at IMD. 'But you may only be interested in one area such as leadership or marketing.'

Equally, you may be unable to take the year or two off work required to do an MBA. Others simply might not need large chunks of MBAs; for example, many bankers will already know much of the financial component.

Alternative programmes broadly fall into two categories – degree and non-degree courses. Those looking to do a degree course could consider a Masters in Finance or Marketing or even, at Warwick Business School, a Masters in Public Administration.

Non-degree courses tend to be shorter (although they can still last several months) and may focus on one or two areas or be a kind of concentrated or taster MBA.

What sort of people take them?

Candidates for shorter business courses may be those who took an MBA 15 years ago and want a refresher. Or they might be individuals in their 20s who want the highlights of an MBA without the huge commitment. 'It's a portfolio approach to executive education,' says Paul Ingram, professor at Columbia Business School. 'A case of what you need when you need it.'

Some courses, such as the four-week Columbia Senior Executive Program (which costs nearly $50,000), focus on things such as leadership and strategy and are tailored for people with more business experience. 'Candidates tend to be 45 to 50 and CEOs or aspiring CEOs,' says Professor Ingram.

Marie Mookini, director of the Sloan Master's Programme at Stanford University (which earns you an MS in Management and costs over $100,000) says: 'Sloans are far more likely to be people with considerable operating experience. In the United States people often go straight from their undergraduate degree to business school. It's a very different environment.'

Are there any other benefits?

Whereas degrees tend to be about building individual capabilities, Mr Stanford says custom courses designed to fit the needs of candidates from a single company can focus on building organizational capabilities. This can allow candidates to build networks across disciplines and functions within companies. 'Sending people from your company on these courses builds bonds. If you have 30 people in a three-week programme, it builds a good community.'

What are the drawbacks?

Obviously non-degree courses do not give you the letters to put after your name and the cachet that goes with them. Other degrees may not have the instant brand recognition that you get with an MBA. That said, as MBAs are so ubiquitous in some areas these days, this could play in your favour.

How to live like a student when you're doing an MBA

Prospective MBA students spend ages agonizing over their career strategy, their goals and choosing the right school and course. But they often spend very little time thinking about what it will be like going back to university and living as a student again.

How should I prepare?

'Insist on speaking not just to current students but also people who studied a year or so ago,' says Rob Yeung, a director of Talentspace and author of *The Extra One Per Cent: How Small Changes Make Exceptional People*. 'They're likely to be able to tell you what works and what doesn't. You should also consider what kind of MBA experience you want. Some MBAs are structured far more like work environments than others.'

How is it likely to differ from being an undergraduate?

'The hardest adjustment isn't the loss of income,' says Fran Langewisch, assistant dean for student affairs at the Kellogg School of Management. 'It's getting into the mode of life. Going back to writing essays and sitting exams is a big change.'

But she says your motivations are often very different and this does make things easier: 'You know why you're here. You're investing in your career.'

Jens Irion, a consultant at Boston Consulting Group who graduated from MIT Sloan in 2008, says: 'Going back to university can give you a chance to step back; it's quite refreshing.'

What is the social life like?

One would assume people in their late 20s and early 30s are more personally settled and mature than 19-year-olds. 'You won't be in the student bar 24/7,' says Aliya Ali-Afzal, MBA career coach at Hult International Business School. 'But MBAs do work hard and play hard and you will need to let off steam.'

Socializing, of course, can be the foundation for all-important networking. 'The social intelligence you gain may be more valuable than the intellectual content and knowledge you pick up,' says Mr Yeung.

What about extra-curricular activities?

Clubs are a big feature of MBA life. 'Some are cultural, some are partners and families, some are volunteering, and some are career related,' says Ms Langewisch. 'There's a lot out there. You could spend your whole time doing extra-curricular stuff.'

Mr Irion was president of the venture capital and private equity club. 'We had 300 members and it was a real highlight,' he says. 'It's fun to run a club and, as they say, it's good for your leadership skills.'

Moreover, even if you shunned sports as an undergraduate, many MBA teams compete with other business school teams and therefore present good opportunities to build camaraderie and relieve tension. Mr Yeung notes: 'Many interviewers are unduly swayed by sporting achievement. They played team sports themselves and they recruit in their own image.'

Even in the most pressurized MBA programmes, there will inevitably be more free time to explore other activities. After all, MBAs do not run all year. 'Our students certainly enjoy the long academic vacations,' says Ms Langewisch. 'Especially if they're American, because US holiday allowances are so small.'

How to stay ahead of the curve

It is a workplace cliché, but what do people really mean when they say you should be ahead of the curve? And how do you get there?

Where do you begin?

Broadly speaking, there are two overlapping aspects to being ahead of the curve. The first is informational: technical knowledge that helps you in your job. The second is personal: everything from networking to gossip to relationships.

Camilla Arnold, global head of coaching at leadership consultancy TXG, explains that you need to begin by saying: '"This is where I want to get to and this is how I want to be perceived. The gap between here and there is this." You should be doing this once or more a year.'

Stephen Viscusi, author of *Bulletproof Your Job*, adds: 'Sit down and write your résumé. If you don't like the way it looks, you should be doing something. Work out what it is.'

How do you deal with the informational side?

You need to step back and think beyond the next meeting agenda. Moreover, you need to do more than just the basic daily routine of keeping up with news in your industry. 'You might look at areas such as politics, economics, society, technology and law,' says Robert Myatt, a director at business psychologists Kaisen. He notes that the internet makes life a lot easier. 'Previously, you had to wade through papers and research. Now you can look at a video of a TED talk.'

You can also set up Google Alerts, not just for you but for key customers, and also follow industry opinion formers on Twitter and so on. Of course, you need to watch out for information overload and be selective. But if you read more about a topic, you develop the right mindset, says Mr Myatt.

How do you deal with the personal side?

You need to make an action plan, says Ms Arnold. 'Ask who and what can help you move forward, then bite the bullet and get on with it,' she says. 'Break it into manageable-sized chunks and work with your personality type... If, for example, you're going to network, you need to think about who you want to meet and what you can bring to the party when you meet them. Rather than throwing business cards around or inviting them on LinkedIn, ask yourself how you can create a meaningful peer relationship.'

Mr Viscusi says you should look at job websites to see who is moving where and what salary they command. 'Don't forget office gossip either,' he adds. 'It tells you things before they happen. Gossip is gold.'

To operate most effectively, he advises: 'Keep up with not only what your boss is doing, but also your boss's boss.'

How do you demonstrate that you are ahead of the curve?

'Make sure your boss knows what you're doing,' says Mr Viscusi.

Ms Arnold agrees. 'If you find something interesting and useful, e-mail your boss. You want them to see you as someone who provides solutions,' he says.

Make yourself the go-to person for whatever your area is.

Mr Viscusi adds: 'When you go in for an appraisal, go in with an up-to-date résumé. This tells them you're prepared – in more ways than one.'

How to benchmark yourself

It is human to worry about how you are doing compared to your colleagues and friends – the workplace equivalent of keeping up with the Joneses. But how do you meaningfully and usefully benchmark your career progress without being obsessive?

How do I take control?

'Recognize that you have to manage your career and if you don't, you run the risk of being left behind,' says Moira Benigson of executive search firm the MBS Group. 'You see people in [big companies] who do a bloody good job, and then one day say: "I've been here 25 years." Automatic promotion no longer happens.'

Ruth Colling, a director at business psychologists Nicholson McBride, adds: 'Ask yourself what success looks like to you. Is it salary? Is it responsibility? Is it the projects you're working on? If you have clear goals, you're more likely to succeed.'

What should I look at?

'A lot of it is being organizationally savvy,' says Ms Colling. 'Recognize that being political is a part of business life. Know what's going on around you.'

Ask yourself if what you are putting in is commensurate with what you are getting out – and if not, why not? Your peers and your boss are the obvious places to start, but you shouldn't limit yourself to them. 'Find a group of people who give you good straight advice,' says executive coach Ros Taylor. This group should extend beyond your company – you want a wide network of contacts, colleagues and friends. Coaches and mentors are also very useful here – this is why they exist. Ms Benigson says headhunters are another excellent resource, especially when it comes to finding out what you are worth. 'Visit an executive search company in your field. Don't just use them when you're looking for a job. Specialist firms will have a good feel for what the market rate for your job is and should be able to offer honest feedback.'

What should I do if I think I am falling behind?

Ms Colling says you should not simply storm into your boss's office and tell them it is not fair. 'Rather you need to think about why others are skipping ahead. Is it because they're better or harder working? Also, what is your objective here – is it to log the fact, make your boss look bad, or get a promotion?'

Ask for feedback if you do not get a job and remember that you cannot always wait for a promotion to come to you. 'Highly successful people often volunteer for things no one else wants to do,' says executive coach Ros Taylor. 'It makes all the difference. You have to put your hand in the air and be a volunteer, not a conscript.'

However, the reasons for your falling behind may be nothing to do with you. For instance, senior people may not be moving on because of the poor economy, or your organization may pay below the market rate – and in cases like these you may well need to move on to get on. Finally, says Ms Benigson: 'Sometimes your face just doesn't fit. If this is true you could leave and fly. You'll be thinking: "My God, why did I stay there so long?"'

Does benchmarking have its limits?

'Remember what motivates people is very different,' says Ms Colling. 'If the thing that motivates you is work–life balance, perhaps you shouldn't be comparing yourself to someone who is motivated by money.'

It is also worth remembering that people progress in very different ways. 'Some people are fantastic at sales but not great managers,' says Ms Benigson. 'In this case, it's OK not to be promoted when others are as long as it's formally recognized that you're very good at what you do and this is reflected in your salary.'

Finally, bear in mind that not all metrics are clear-cut indicators of your progress: a colleague may earn more than you for no reason other than that they drive a harder bargain.

Chapter Nine
Practical ways to get ahead

Returning from maternity leave

Returning from maternity leave is one of the toughest career transitions women face. Not only do you come back after a significant break; you come back to reduced flexibility, increased demands and a different set of priorities.

What should I do before I go back?

'Everyone worries about "baby brain",' says Ruth Colling, a director at Nicholson McBride, the business psychologists. 'So you need to start preparing mentally before you return.' Chris Parke, managing director of Talking Talent, a consultancy that specializes in coaching women, agrees: 'A good place to start is to think about your key stakeholders. Ensure you stay in touch with them and speak to them before you go back, to see what has changed.' Ms Colling says it might be a good idea to ask for a kind of 'return to work interview' to pin down your objectives.

How do I deal with my changed priorities?

'Recognize that you have a less elastic day and prioritize ruthlessly,' says Geraldine Gallacher, a coach at Executive Coaching. 'Becoming a mother is actually very good practice for this. You need to focus on doing what you're good at and not sweat the small stuff.' On the baby side, Lisa Hart, a recently returned mother and chief executive of Acritas, a market research company, says you need to expect to be very tired. 'Colleagues are unlikely to really understand this. You just have to tell yourself it doesn't last forever and deal with it.'

How do I deal with not being able to stay at work late?

'Sometimes women feel very self-conscious that they're not available,' says Ms Gallacher, 'and they get defensive and sound almost militant about having to leave on time. Don't do this – just leave when you have to and be firm about it. People will accept it.'

What about working part time?

The recession has been quite helpful here. Women doing four days a week or less used to feel that they had be moved on to the 'mummy track'. But during the past few years, a lot of companies have been using reduced hours as an alternative to redundancy, so the connection between part-time work and motherhood is breaking down. But resist the urge to arrange important work calls on your day with your child.

What about my own expectations?

You need to manage your own perceptions too, says Mr Parke. 'First, you need to ensure that you're not focusing on survival and that you're going in the direction you want to. If you've decided to slow your career down, you need to deal with your concerns that colleagues will overtake you.' Self-belief is critical too, says Ms Colling. 'You can be a lawyer and a mother – believe it. Doubt can become a self-fulfilling prophecy.'

Are there any career upsides?

'Having a child gives you a bit of life perspective and makes you clear about expectations,' says Ms Gallacher. 'So in some ways it can be pretty useful. It's a bit of a stereotype but women often think they have to cover all the bases, whereas men focus on big ideas. This can be an early wake-up call for female high achievers.'

How to ask for a pay rise

With confidence still fragile and money tight and other opportunities hard to come by, extra money is no longer a question of acting like you have itchy feet. So how do you ask for a pay rise?

When should I ask?

'People don't really like to ask for pay rises so they usually wait until an external catalyst such as a new baby, a partner earning more or even a falling out with a colleague causes a kind of tipping point,' says Rosemary Smart of Penna, the HR consulting group. 'It's probably better not to wait until you get to that point.'

How should I prepare?

'Consider the balance of power,' says John McMillan, senior partner at Scotwork, a negotiation skills consultancy. 'How much do you need the job and how much do they need you? If there's a queue of unemployed people who can do your job, that probably doesn't strengthen your hand.'

Make sure you understand your company's pay structure and its review system. Look at where you are against your objectives. And, of course, research the market rate for your role.

In addition, you should make a list of everything else about your job that matters. With work, money is a bit like beauty: it is initially very attractive, but the rest of the job is the personality that you live with every day.

Sarah Sweetman of Organizational Edge, the business psychologists, adds that you need to be confident of your ground: 'If you can't convince yourself your case is watertight, then you shouldn't try it on your boss.'

How should I present my argument?

'For me, the crux of this is about couching your case in value,' says Ms Sweetman. 'Old arguments such as length of service, loyalty and cost of living won't get you very far. You need to demonstrate your value – possibly even in cash terms – to the business. You have to explain why the business is better off for having you and how you're distinctive compared to other people.'

You should also bring in your aspirations and explain where you see your career going. These all form part of your personal narrative and are what make you compelling: they will help your boss see why you will be of greater value in the future – and why you should be encouraged to stay now.

What about horse trading?

In the current climate, employers are unlikely to give you a rise just for being you. 'Be willing to give something in order to get something,' says Mr McMillan. 'For example, you might say: "If you give me a rise, then I'll mentor some of the younger staff."'

Ms Smart adds that even if you do not get a pay rise, there are other ways of getting what you want. 'You might say: "If you can't give me a rise, might there be some form of discretionary bonus," or "I'm not happy working 60 hours a week. If you can't pay me more, can I work fewer hours?"'

What about jam tomorrow?

There is nothing necessarily wrong with this, especially in these straitened times. 'You might say that if I meet these goals, you'll give me X per cent,' says Mr McMillan.

But you have to make sure that, come tomorrow, you really do get what you have been promised. If not, the next question you need to ask yourself is: 'Can I afford to leave – and can I afford not to?'

Working for an interim boss

Your manager might be the single most important person in your working life, but how do you work for someone who you know isn't in it for the long run?

Are there different kinds of temporary boss?

If you have someone standing in for a few weeks, matters are pretty straightforward and it is no different to your boss being on holiday. Real interim management – such as that covering maternity leave or months between permanent bosses – is more complex.

Ian Gooden, chief operating officer of human resources consultancy Chiumento, says that there are two main reasons to bring in an interim manager. 'The first is in a kind of bridging role and their remit tends to be care and maintenance and not to rock the boat. The second is someone who has been brought in to get something done and often something uncomfortable such as a reorganization.'

What should my first moves be?

'Sit down and have a proper conversation,' says Rob Yeung, a psychologist at Talentspace, a leadership consulting firm. 'See what style they have and how it fits with what you're used to. Explain how you're used to working, but don't say "This is the way things are done." Rather, say "This is how it was – is that acceptable to you?"'

Mr Gooden says you need to understand their agenda: 'It won't always be apparent. But the nature of your relationship with them may be very dependent on why they were brought in. Ask the right questions and do a lot of listening. Be politically astute.'

What should I expect?

'The challenge is to manage your own expectations,' says Mr Gooden. 'It may be unrealistic to expect deep and meaningful discussions about your career. It can be very frustrating, but you need to accept certain things probably won't happen while they're in charge.'

However, executive coach Geraldine Gallacher says there are upsides. She suggests you offer to attend high-profile meetings on their behalf. Alternatively, she says it could be the perfect opportunity 'to arm someone with a loaded gun and stand back as they shoot down some sacred cows in need of culling'.

What are the pitfalls?

'It's counterproductive to think "What's the point in investing time in this person who isn't going to be around for long?"' says Ms Gallacher.

'Don't assume anything,' says Mr Yeung. 'If the interim manager is covering maternity leave, the person in question may not return. So make an effort and focus on their good qualities even if you preferred your old boss.'

What can I gain?

Mr Gooden says interim managers can make useful allies, particularly if they've been brought in to make big changes and you've helped them do so.

Mr Yeung adds that they tend to be highly regarded people who move around a lot: 'If you make a good impression, instead of you looking for your next job, your next job may come to you.'

How to make a temporary contract into a permanent job

Many people are happy to work on a temporary or contract basis. But if you want something longer term, how do you convince your employer you are worth hanging on to?

How do I start the process?

Focus on doing the temporary job well first. 'Get in there, understand what is expected of you and really deliver,' says David Fleming, a director at professional services recruiter Badenoch & Clark. 'You need to start proving that you are indispensable before you start looking for opportunities. Do the basics well, too – know the dress code and the values, be punctual and polite, and go in with the attitude that you need to prove yourself.'

How do I ensure any permanent roles come my way?

'Make an effort to build relationships so that if a permanent position arises, people think of you,' says Mr Fleming.

Think beyond the team you are on, says Sue Smith, a director at BIE Interim. 'Talk to the HR department – they might have something elsewhere in the business. Get to know how the business works and make people aware of what you have been doing.'

Your networking should extend outside the company too, since partners and suppliers are all potential sources of longer-term employment.

Jane Barrett, career coach and co-author of *If Not Now, When? How to Take Charge of Your Career*, says: 'If you are nearing the end of your contract, you need to think like a consultant: what are the other things you could do to improve company performance? Write a proposal – essentially you are trying to create a job for yourself.'

Some companies take on contract workers as a way of finding permanent staff. 'People are less willing to conduct expensive searches at the moment,' says Ms Smith. 'They take on temporary people, then offer them something more if it goes in the right direction.'

Ms Barrett adds: 'It's a little bit like a first date.'

Can I ask for a job, and what arguments can I use?

Choose your moment, says Mr Fleming. After you have built a rapport, 'If someone congratulates you on a job well done or asks you how it's going, that's a good time to ask. Start by saying you really enjoy working there.'

Ms Barrett says: 'If you have been somewhere six months, you will understand where you can add value and you have a proven track record. The likelihood is so much higher of it working out on both sides.'

Why might a company be wary of making a temp permanent?

'If you have been temping for 10 years, companies might be a bit cautious,' says Ms Barrett. 'They worry that you'll struggle to fit into the culture and with the bureaucracy.'

She adds that in a downturn they might be concerned that you are simply looking for a safe haven and, when the economic storm ends, you will go temporary again. 'If you've been [temping] for a long time, you'll really need to convince them.'

How to leapfrog a superior

There are few greater sources of frustration in your ascent up the corporate ladder than having it blocked by someone who shows no signs of moving on. However, a flat economy means that this scenario is all too common. So what can you do about it?

Where should I begin?

Start by talking to people – a mentor, coach, or people above the person in question, suggests Neil Roden, human resources consulting partner at PwC, the professional services firm. 'But, rather than complain about them, make the discussion about you and the issues for your career.'

Robert Myatt, a director at Kaisen, the business psychologists, says, 'A lot of organizations recognize that this is a problem – and they are trying to ensure that high-potential [employees] feel they have a future. So ask if there is a fast-track programme.'

The one thing you shouldn't do is dwell on the impasse, says executive coach Ros Taylor. 'There are always things you can do.'

What about moving sideways?

'Look sideways and at secondments,' says Ms Taylor. 'Many CEOs have had dozens of jobs in the same company; having been in lots of different departments can be a real plus.'

Even though a horizontal move might be at the same grade, says Mr Myatt, 'it can still be a step up in terms of scope of responsibility and building your reputation and capabilities. Think broadly about where you could take your skills and see it as a long game. What you do next might not be the ideal job but it could open up possibilities.'

What else can I do?

'Develop your reputation in other parts of the organization,' says Mr Myatt. 'Make sure the right people know the right things about you.'

Mr Roden says: 'Get known as someone who gets things done. Senior managers like doers. You also have to be slightly street smart about how to promote yourself and get yourself noticed.'

What about small companies?

A career block may seem more problematic in small companies, which don't have dozens of business units and locations. But Mr Myatt says: 'In a small company there's often more latitude to create opportunities to expand your current role; there can be more informal opportunities. If you can make a business case, you can often create the role for yourself.' Ms Taylor adds: 'Be entrepreneurial, proactive and energetic. If you have a good idea, people will often put you in charge of it.'

Can I leapfrog the person above me?

'You might get parachuted in above people or leapfrog them – if others believe you have a lot of potential,' says Mr Roden. 'You may even propose restructuring around the role.' Many people who leapfrog those above them feel awkward in their relationship with their former superior. But they shouldn't. 'Don't make a big deal of it,' says Ms Taylor. 'Just have a conversation with the person and say "We need to work together." It's usually absolutely fine.'

How to change sector

Many people are fairly relaxed about changing jobs. But what about leaving not just your employer but the industry you have been working in? Is it a good way of getting out of your comfort zone or a step too far?

Why might I want to change sectors?

You might be unsatisfied in your field or feel you need new challenges. Or you might want to broaden your CV and gain experience of different areas. You may even have a burning desire to work in a particular area.

What are the benefits?

In the short term, changing industries can reinvigorate your career and offer new challenges. In the longer term, it can add real value. 'If you look at senior executives you'll often see a range of sectoral experience,' says Elisabeth Marx, a director of Stonehaven Executive Search. 'Having made lateral or sectoral moves shows you're adaptable and changeable and can perform well in a variety of different scenarios. It's similar to having worked in several countries; it reduces your riskiness from a prospective employer's point of view.'

How do I go about it?

'Really think about what your interests are and what you're good at,' says Catherine Roan, managing director of career change experts Careershifters.org.

'Be very blue sky about it. Then start talking to people. Even with very drastic changes, the majority of people will get their new role by networking.'

Whatever you do, do not just jump in. 'We see lots of examples of people who don't do their research and wind up just as miserable in a new sector,' she says.

How difficult is it?

Needless to say, this kind of change will require considerable drive on your part and quite possibly the support of family and friends. You should also be prepared for a steep learning curve. No matter how good you are in your current role, there are likely to be very basic things you will not know in your new one. 'You want your new organization to have a decent [induction] programme and it's good to have a specific mentor,' says Ms Marx.

How do I leverage my skills from my previous sector?

'The key points are relevance and impact,' says Tony Sheehan, learning services director at Ashridge Business School and a former engineer at Arup. 'It's the ability to bring all your knowledge to work rather than just your label. Often, when you change sector, you'll bring experience that isn't common and a new way of looking at things.'

He points out that people sometimes value you for skills that come from outside work altogether. 'At Arup, we had an administrative assistant who'd previously worked for a veterinarian and enjoyed horse riding. Even though her title was administrative assistant, she was our equestrian expert and probably worked and advised on 20 equestrian projects.'

Ms Marx adds: 'There are parallels and overlaps between sectors, especially if you're moving into the same functional role, but it would be riskier to change role, sector and organization all at once.'

Nonetheless, Ms Roan stresses that anything is possible: 'We've worked with an IT consultant who is now a guide on expeditions to the Arctic.'

How to follow a failure

If a great predecessor is a hard act to follow, does that make someone who has been a failure an easy act to follow? Or do you need to be wary you don't repeat their mistakes?

What should I do before I take the job?

'The first thing to do is really analyse the reasons for your predecessor's failure,' says Elisabeth Marx, a partner at Stonehaven, an executive recruitment firm. 'Did they have the wrong skill set? Was the job different to what they agreed upon? Were the resources there, and was the person given the freedom they needed to do their job?'

Ms Marx says you need to be able to understand what you can change. An important question you should ask is whether your predecessor was a one-off: 'If the role has a high turnover, you should be asking questions.'

What should I do if I take the job?

Robert Myatt, a director at business psychologists Kaisen, says: 'You need to clean the place up, literally and figuratively. If someone visits your department, you want them to see the difference. Move quickly and make a clean break.'

Executive coach Ros Taylor takes a similar view: 'You need to do some distancing. Then you need to visit your major stakeholders. Show them that you're efficient and that relationships with you will be different.'

However, Ms Marx warns that you should not be too hasty. 'You may be under huge pressure to make changes very fast, but this kind of situation actually needs focus and time.'

How should I deal with those who report to me?

'People's confidence and morale will have taken a battering,' says Mr Myatt. 'Make them feel valued and relate what they are doing to a bigger purpose.'

Ms Marx adds that, as well as being demoralized, some members of your team may have been left deeply cynical. 'Some of them may also need to be replaced,' she says. 'If you need to get rid of people, do it as quickly as possible. It is a period of high anxiety and you need to re-energize the environment around you and give people aspirational goals.'

How do I refer to the problems of the past?

'If someone has left as a failure, the smart thing to do is not to refer to incompetence. Don't personalize failure,' says Ms Marx.

Mr Myatt says: 'Get people to start looking to the future rather than dwelling on the past. Paint a picture of what the world will look like and create a feeling of optimism.

'If you do talk about the past, try to find the good. Rather than look at the negatives, look for times when things were going right. Ask, can you recreate that again?'

You should also be generous and resist the urge to bash the previous incumbent, even when it is easy and obvious.

Nonetheless, Mr Myatt points out that you should also recognize that other people may want to vent and you should not stop them doing so. 'Do let them recognize that things weren't great and talk about it.'

Applying for internal positions

Applying for a job where nobody knows you can sometimes be easier than looking for one where you already work. How do you best handle the pros and cons of familiarity?

How do I seek and find vacant positions?

Steph Oerton, head of colleague development at Cable & Wireless Worldwide, says that in large organizations you should build up networks to bring opportunities to you. 'Broaden your knowledge of the organization, make contacts outside your business area, make yourself known and raise your profile.' Ms Oerton also suggests finding mentors across the organization and letting those above you know that you're ambitious. 'These people can signpost opportunities for you.'

What might count in my favour?

'Internal people are seen as lower risk,' explains Ms Oerton. 'And one great advantage is that, as an internal candidate, you can really do in-depth research on the role.'

This could include talking not just to the position's incumbent but also those who have done the job in the past.

You can also direct your research efforts on yourself: if your internal performance reviews are good, get hold of them and press them into use.

'Getting hold of an internal recommendation can work wonders,' adds interview coach Margaret Buj. 'Especially if your experience isn't a 100 per cent match for the job.'

Needless to say, you should make sure you ask them first.

What should I watch out for in the interview?

Ms Buj says you should go in with the same attitude you would for an external interview; you may know your interviewer well but you should expect far more than a friendly chat. 'For senior jobs you may also be interviewed by a panel of five or six people and you're unlikely to know them all,' she says.

Even if your interviewer is your line manager, do not presume they know everything about you, says Peter Shaw, author of *Defining Moments: Navigating Through Business and Organisational Life.* 'It's really important to talk up your accomplishments. Help other people remember what you've done. Also, say things with clarity. If you're moving internally, you know a lot about issues and so on. But you still need to say it. Be explicit about the experience and strengths you have and how they fit the role, even if you think it's obvious.'

Mr Shaw warns that although internal candidates are known quantities, they might also be dismissed as the safe option. 'You need to show real passion. Be clear that you want the job. Internal people can sometimes be half-hearted and interviewers may see them as a bit boring. They want someone who really wants the job.'

Am I likely to encounter any political difficulties?

It goes without saying that you should tell your manager you are applying for a new position internally as they are likely to find out anyway.

A common difficulty is being asked to critique a department by those who run it – especially if they are in your chain of command. 'You should talk in terms of opportunities and challenges rather than saying you're a grotty bunch of leaders,' advises Mr Shaw.

Because applying for jobs internally can be easier, Ms Oerton says people sometimes overdo it. 'Internal people sometimes take a scattergun approach and apply for a lot of jobs. This can make it look like they don't want to be in their own role, so you need to have clarity about what it is you want to do and what you're looking for.'

It is worth remembering that your own company is likely to know you, warts and all. 'You need to remember everything you do will have impacted someone somewhere down the line,' she adds.

How to cope with being passed over for promotion

You have your eye on a big promotion only for the prize to go to someone else. How do you deal with this?

Do not give in to anger

'It's incredibly hard not to be resentful,' says Jane Clarke, a director of business psychologists Nicholson McBride. 'Most people are. You need to fight this. If you are angry, you get into a vicious circle, where you confirm the choice of the person who didn't promote you. Instead, you need to put yourself in a position where it doesn't happen again.'

She advises you to start by calmly and coolly reviewing the situation yourself.

After the disappointment, what next?

'The best way to look at it is that it's a really good opportunity for feedback,' says Corinne Mills, managing director of Personal Career Management. 'Ask the person to be as honest as possible. You might have just missed it or you could have been miles off. It's a good reality check.'

She adds that you should do something proactive like asking for more experience or a coach. 'You should also think about your relationship with the person who gets the job, especially if it's an old peer,' adds Ms Clarke. 'You need to be seen as helpful and supportive and constructive.'

Even if it is a loathed colleague, you need to clear the air and put your new relationship on as good a footing as possible.

What are the reasons I didn't get the job?

The most obvious one is that you were up against people better qualified or more experienced than you. But this isn't always the case. 'In large companies it may just be political, and they could have promoted the less able person,' says Moira Benigson of the MBS group, an executive search firm. 'Sometimes when this happens it is worth hanging around as the wrong person doesn't last long.'

It is worth bearing in mind that, during a recession, many decisions can become arbitrary.

Ms Benigson adds that you need to be as informed as possible: 'Watch what's happening to colleagues – who's closer to the board, who's privy to more meetings? Never rule out talking to headhunters. Keep abreast of tangible information.'

When should I consider my position?

'You may get the sense that they thought "No way on this earth" and sometimes your face just doesn't fit,' says Ms Mills. 'In that case, you need to get that promotion elsewhere.'

Ms Clarke adds: 'If you're passed over more than once, you should ask yourself, "Realistically, does this organization have concerns about me?"'

In big organizations, you may be able to move internally; in smaller ones, an external move may be the only choice. 'Never stay because you're afraid to leave,' says Ms Benigson. 'Sometimes, if you know you're not going to get the job, it may be a good idea to leave pre-emptively.'

So should I just shy away from internal promotions?

'It's always a risk to go for internal promotions,' says Ms Mills. 'If you're successful, you may be managing former colleagues and if you're not successful people will talk.' But, she adds, it is nearly always a risk worth taking. 'It says you want to get ahead and you're ambitious.'

Returning to a former employer

Starting a new job is always stressful. But what if you are returning to an organization that you have worked at before? Do your pre-existing relationships make it easier or harder?

Does the company matter?

Multinationals are often so big that you may return to a different subsidiary and know nobody. Similarly, if the time gap is long enough, you will, in effect, be returning to a different company. Returning really becomes an issue in medium-sized or smaller organizations or when you return to the same part of a larger company within a comparatively short time.

How will people view me?

'With somewhere completely new, you can reinvent yourself,' says Graham Abbey, an executive coach at March Friday.

'If you're returning, it's about the nature of pre-existing relationships and how you re-establish them. You have all those things you said at your leaving party.'

Robert Myatt, a director at Kaisen, the business psychologists, adds: 'You may need to rebuild bridges. People have a tendency to be slightly critical and disparaging of those who have left because they have become outsiders. So you need to rebuild that trust and that sense of being an insider.'

What should I not do?

'Avoid the temptation to harp on about what it was like beforehand,' says Owen Morgan, a director at Penna, the human resources consultancy. 'It will only put people's backs up. In the intervening period, things will have changed. People will have changed and the culture will have changed.'

Mr Myatt adds: 'Organizations aren't interested in how things were – you want to look like part of the future, not part of the past.'

Mr Abbey stresses the need to be open-minded. 'You need to think about the baggage you're taking in,' he says. 'When you've worked somewhere, you know it, warts and all – but how accurate is that picture now? You need to be careful of making assumptions.'

What if I'm returning at a higher level?

'If you've gone out to get more experience and always thought you might come back, your return can be a very positive story,' says Mr Morgan. 'But you shouldn't cast yourself as a returning conquering hero.'

You need to remember that other people have moved on too – and you should not be seen to be belittling their achievements. 'If anything, be more agreeable than necessary – show a bit of humility,' says Mr Myatt.

What if I return under something of a cloud?

Ideally, if you left in a blaze of glory to seek your fortune, you should not be back if your firework turned out to be a damp squib. But with the economy far from buoyant, people do find themselves returning in circumstances not of their choosing. 'Be open about it,' says Mr Myatt. 'If you try to hide your reasons, people will be more suspicious.'

Are there any upsides?

'People forget that a lot of success in your career depends on the networks you make,' says Mr Abbey. 'If you go somewhere new, the "set-up" costs are very high but, if you return to a business, you may already have a very well developed network.' It's worth remembering too that many organizations recognize that good staff do return and it should be encouraged – Bain, McKinsey and Allen & Overy are all examples of companies with alumni networks.

Working abroad

A stint overseas is seen by many as an important addition to your CV – and by some organizations as essential experience for senior management. But how do you ensure that it really works to your advantage?

What should I consider before I go?

'Think strategically about the position,' says executive coach Nicola Bunting. 'Does it fit in with your career goals or are you being seduced by the glamour? Also before you go, you need to have a re-entry plan. You don't want to compromise on the role you take when you come back.'

Kevan Hall, chief executive of the international people management group, Global Integration, says you shouldn't underestimate the culture shock. 'Go out there beforehand. See what you're getting into.'

What are the likely career upsides and downsides?

Nigel Parslow, UK managing director of Harvey Nash Executive Search, says staying put may not be an option for organizations that have a strong overseas presence. He adds that the experience you gain is also very attractive. In *Breaking Through Culture Shock: What You Need to Succeed in International Business*, Elisabeth Marx notes that 82 per cent of the managers she interviewed reported positive effects on their professional lives, such as more responsibility and being more marketable.

However, says Mr Hall, out of sight can mean out of mind. 'Those who are closer to the centre of power do tend to get noticed more and progress faster. If you're remote, it's not enough to do a good job, you need to work on your visibility and network. Some people even have a mentor back at the head office.' Visiting home often can also help – as well as smoothing your eventual return.

What are the personal considerations?

The biggest is family. This can be particularly hard for people in the middle of their careers who may have children at school. Ms Bunting says: 'There's your partner's career too. Some people's spouses try and commute back and I'd really advise against this as it makes an already stressful situation even more difficult.' It can be very hard for non-working partners who do not have the ready-made network provided by the office. 'Your financial package should reflect what you're giving up,' she says.

For those moving to a more expensive country, there may be significant lifestyle changes. Indian middle managers, for instance, may be used to domestic help.

What about destination?

Mr Hall says: 'There's been a power shift to Asia, and that, coupled with low growth in America and Europe, means that particularly if you're an ambitious young thing you might want to spend some time there.' He adds that if you're in China or Japan you will probably only experience that market, whereas in Singapore or Hong Kong you will get more regional experience.

Is there an ideal length of time?

Many people say two to three years. But this will vary according to the country and organization. Obviously, for an American, the UK is relatively easy to slot into, but in Japan the language barrier would make it harder to settle in. Mr Parslow adds that if you spend too long abroad, you can wind up with a not entirely positive expat label attached to you.

How to come out of retirement

For many people, retirement is no longer the career full stop it once was. But what are the considerations for those wishing to re-enter the workforce after retiring?

Why do people come out of retirement?

'Perhaps surprisingly, the reasons people give for going back to work are usually non-financial,' says Nic Peeling, author of *Brilliant Retirement*. 'You might be a bit bored or miss the stimulation and challenges of work.'

Early retirees might have discovered that they no longer fancy 30 years of gardening and travel. 'Very talented people are often missed from the marketplace,' says career coach John Lees. 'If people keep offering you interesting things, it can be hard to resist.'

How do you prepare?

'Assess yourself and put together a plan,' says Willma Tucker, a consultant at Right Management. 'Often people can use retirement as a way to rebalance their priorities. Look at your lifestyle, relationships and money issues. Think about what it is you enjoy.'

Writing a CV can be a good way of crystallizing these things. 'Sell yourself as someone who can bring experience without being inflexible or set in their ways,' says Mr Peeling.

You should also tap your network. 'You're more likely to get something through someone you know,' says Mr Lees. 'Talk to people in your age range who've found different ways of working.'

What sort of roles should people look for?

'If you're looking for a job with security, it can be hard,' says Mr Peeling. 'But if you're not looking for a full-time, permanent position it is a lot easier. Consulting is the obvious route for middle and upper management. You're very low risk to the company and you can charge a surprising amount.'

You have much greater freedom over the mix of work you do. 'You might choose to do a combination of paid and voluntary,' says Mr Lees. 'You could say, "I'll work these months of the year" or 'I'll do these parts of the job."'

What should people watch out for?

'Many retired people will be very overqualified for the jobs they're applying for,' says Mr Peeling. 'Don't lie on your CV about how talented and senior you were.'

Mr Lees says people may question your commitment: 'You must convince people that you're returning for the right reasons. If you don't need the money they may be wary, so you should have a clear and valid message as to why you're going back.'

Companies also tend to worry about older people and technology, so ensure your IT skills are up to speed and join LinkedIn.

You need to be aware of job creep too. Talented people who take on lower-level or part-time jobs often find these roles growing to become like the ones they retired from.

What about starting a business?

'Starting a company based on a hobby is also common and you hear a surprising number of success stories,' says Mr Peeling. 'You get really interesting things like bespoke kites.'

He cautions against ventures with high capital risks, while Ms Tucker adds: 'Setting up a business can easily take over your life.'

How to deal with being underworked

For many stressed-out executives, having too little to do might seem like a dream come true. But being underworked can make you anxious in the short term and, in the long run, damage your career.

Is it really a problem?

'Being underemployed is almost as stressful as being overworked,' says Graham Abbey, an executive coach at March Friday, a management consultancy. 'You find yourself struggling to find things to do and you start to doubt yourself. Not being utilized, challenged and stretched to some degree is not a good position to be in. It's not actually comfortable.'

Moreover, in the long term, it devalues you as your skills, capabilities and confidence will erode. 'Coasting for any length of time is a risk,' says Ceri Roderick, a partner at business psychologists Pearn Kandola. 'You miss opportunities.'

Where should I start?

First, take stock: ask yourself how big a problem it really is. 'Whatever situation we're in, we tend to think that it will last forever,' says Octavius Black of the Mind Gym. 'It usually doesn't.'

Equally, you should also ensure you are not missing something. 'You don't want a nasty shock when you discover you haven't been doing everything expected of you,' says Mr Abbey. 'Part of the challenge is keeping yourself going,' adds Mr Black. 'You don't want to let what you still have to do expand to fill your time, because having spare time can be a big opportunity.'

Is it cyclical?

'Lots of jobs are quite volatile in terms of workload,' says Mr Abbey. 'If yours is, try to think of it as annualized hours – as in I'm not busy right now but in three weeks time I'll be working 12-hour days. If this is the case, use the time to recover and catch up.'

If you are in this position, it is a good idea to reach an understanding with your boss that in quiet times you are allowed to be absent for a few hours. 'In cyclical jobs, use your quiet time to maximize productivity for the next time you're working hard,' says Mr Roderick. 'Some people simply chill and others develop themselves. But you can learn to chill out – and it's not a bad idea to do so.'

What should I do if it is a medium- or long-term problem?

If your lack of work is structural, there could be a number of reasons. The obvious one is that there isn't enough work around. But Mr Abbey notes that it can also happen when your capability improves. 'Suddenly, you find you can do your job in 60 per cent of the time.'

If it is a medium-term problem, Mr Black says you should use it to build up your capability. 'Come up with ideas and research the market,' he suggests. 'Build up your emotional bank account. Do favours for people with your spare time. No matter how small it is. They'll feel they owe you one.'

If it's a long-term issue, you should speak to your boss as it is better to tell them you're underworked than have them tell you. Mr Roderick advises going to your boss with a solution. 'Say, "I have spare time and I could do this," rather than "I don't have enough to do."'

Whatever the case, says Mr Roderick, you cannot slack forever. 'You always get found out eventually and if you've been doing it for years, you can really have the rug pulled from under you.'

Being overqualified for the job

With a stale economy, fluid careers and work–life concerns, many people now find themselves applying for jobs for which they are overqualified. How do you deal with having more than it takes?

How should I sell myself?

Go in with the attitude you would have at any interview – that this is a job you want and you are showing your best side. 'Demonstrate enthusiasm,' says Peter Shaw, an executive coach at Praesta. 'Don't be apologetic or embarrassed about your qualifications – it will sound like you don't want the job. But don't draw unnecessary attention to them or oversell yourself either… Show that you'll be a good team member and build rapport.'

Hannah Stratford, head of business psychology at human resources consultants ETS, says that many people take lesser jobs to get into their ideal companies, and there is no harm in saying so.

What are the problems likely to be?

'Some employers might be nervous that in a tough economy, you're looking for any port in a storm,' says Ian Gooden, chief operating officer of HR consultancy Chiumento. 'You need to have a very compelling story and demonstrate clear career logic in your move.'

Mr Shaw says to be mindful that if you are being interviewed by your future manager, your experience might make them nervous.

'Don't give the impression you want to unseat the boss – they could feel quite threatened, like they are hiring a competitor. Instead, show you care about the success of the organization.'

How do I sell it to myself?

'The career ladder has had its day,' says Mr Gooden. 'Careers now have ups and downs and most people will be faced with a change of direction at some point. Sometimes, you need to go backwards to go forwards.'

Remember that good people, wherever they are, rise quickly. Try to think about your move holistically – you may see more of friends and family, you will be more relaxed and you might be doing a job that is more genuinely interesting to you personally. Also bear in mind that management is not for everyone, especially in vocations such as law, engineering and the creative industries, where the technical side is often the attraction.

How do I show commitment?

It is realistic for a company to worry that someone who is over-qualified might jump ship if something better comes along, so you need to convince them otherwise. 'If you know that the organization has certain things to deliver over the next year, show how you will help and contribute,' says Mr Shaw. But, he adds, you should not tell untruths. 'If you don't plan on staying a long time, be honest. Most organizations would prefer someone good who will stay for a year to someone mediocre who will stay for three.'

Ms Stratford also says you should ask about the organization's fast-track policies. 'This demonstrates ambition, while reassuring the employer that you are serious about progressing at the company.'

What about salary?

'Ask how the pay scale at the company reflects high performance,' says Ms Stratford. 'This demonstrates confidence in your ability to succeed in this role and can allow you to get a better idea of exactly what is on offer.' She adds that it's important to look at the whole package too, not just the base salary as benefits and bonus can all add up. However, says Mr Shaw, 'You need to be realistic. If you stand on ceremony too much, you may wind up unemployed or in a job you hate.' Mr Gooden adds that those who are downshifting need to think about salary in the context of their lives too. 'It might be nice not to have to worry about X and Y, but you could just be swapping these worries for worries about how to pay the school fees. Some people who take a salary cut discover they're far more materialistic than they'd realized.'

Being thrown in at the deep end

Being thrown in at the deep end at work can be terrifying but it's also a great opportunity to advance your career. So how do you ensure that you swim rather than sink?

How do I deal with feeling overwhelmed?

'It's so tempting to end up drowning in the detail,' says Geraldine Gallacher, an executive coach. 'You can get distracted by the newness of everything and forget to breathe, so it is vital to create space by looking above and beyond your immediate situation and remind yourself of your goals.'

Jenny Ungless, a career coach and the author of *Shine*, says: 'The first thing is, don't panic. The fact of the matter is that you've been promoted because someone thinks you're capable.'

It's also a matter of getting yourself in the right mindset, says business psychologist Jean Roberts. 'I always tell people to recite the mantra: if you believe it'll work, you'll see opportunities, otherwise you'll see obstacles.'

How do I get up to speed?

'Know what your boss's priorities are,' Ms Ungless says. 'Have a meeting to clarify what your line manager wants and what you'll be measured on... For the first couple of weeks you have permission to ask stupid questions, so gather information and get as clear a picture as possible.'

Ms Roberts says: 'Acknowledge you don't know everything and that you're looking for help and support. Consult widely. It can be tempting just to get out there and do something. But do take a minute to think about what you're doing and make sure you're heading in the right direction.'

How do I start making my mark?

'In any new job, there's a window of about 100 days in which you succeed or fail,' says Ms Gallacher. 'When a company or department is in a mess when you arrive, it's vital to act fast but beware of making radical changes without really checking out your facts, which means you need to listen, although it may be "speed listening."'

That said, there is nothing wrong with identifying a few 'easy wins' – these will boost your confidence and standing, and help you appear to be in control. Ms Roberts says you must consider how you can be most effective. 'Look at who you are and where you can make the most impressive contribution. Try to work out what matters and don't waste time engaging in areas where you have no influence,' she says.

How do I convince my team I'm in control?

The best way is to provide them with unambiguous evidence. But there is much you can do while you amass this evidence. 'Talk to people and get their input,' says Ms Ungless. 'But make decisions too. You want to be seen as not afraid to make decisions. People respect those who put themselves on the line.'

Ms Gallacher says that, as well as bonding with underlings and superiors, you should also build strong lateral relationships with your peers. 'They can often scupper the best-laid plans as most change needs a coordinated response.'

A big internal move

Changing jobs within an organization can be as significant as going elsewhere, especially if you work for a large business. But how do you approach a new role that isn't quite a blank slate?

What should I consider before moving?

Check that your company takes internal promotion seriously. 'Ask yourself about the culture of the organization,' says Elisabeth Marx, a partner at Stonehaven Executive Search. 'Look at the executive team – if everyone's external, that's a problem. The good news is, many companies have got a lot better at this... Organizations recognize that at a senior level, internal promotion is considerably less risky.'

As for whether the role makes sense in terms of your career, Ms Marx adds: 'You should look for challenging assignments such as turnrounds, growing a business and new markets, especially if they're international. Ask yourself if you're being tested. Is the role critical for the business and is it a key area for the future?'

Don't get hung up on job titles: grade and responsibility are more important than words on a business card.

What are my advantages as an internal candidate?

'Even if it's a big move, you'll still have the advantage of your internal network,' says Jenny Ungless, author of *Career Ahead: The Complete Career Handbook*. 'Make this point when you're going for the job. Say: "I know these people. They will help me get things done."'

Internal candidates are also better placed to find out what their new boss is really like, why the last person left and what is really expected of them.

How should I approach the role?

'Treat it like a new job,' says executive coach Geraldine Gallacher. 'It's tempting to let projects from the old job hang over into the new role but this is a mistake because you end up doing neither success-fully. It's vital that you negotiate a clean exit and entry into the new role with a fixed deadline for when you start. If anything, you should start working on the new job while you're still on the old one rather than the other way around.'

Ms Gallacher adds that although internal candidates are less likely to have a formal induction period, you should use your first few weeks to understand your stakeholders' expectations and get any stupid questions out of the way.

What about money?

'If it's a senior position the organization will probably have adver-tised externally, so the pay scale will have been made public,' says Ms Ungless. 'But, as an internal candidate, you can push for the higher end of the range. Say, "I know the corporate culture. There's less training. I can hit the ground running."'

However, Ms Gallacher notes that you are not taking the same risk as an external candidate so you need to be realistic. 'Having seen a number of external candidates and their pay demands, your company may see you as much better value for money and this might have swung the decision your way,' she says.

Chapter Ten
Slightly more abstract ways to get ahead

How to replace a hero

Any promotion forces you to redouble your efforts to impress, and this is especially true when your predecessor was respected, admired and even loved. So how do you deal with the inevitable comparisons? How do you put your own stamp on things? How do you step into big shoes?

How should I prepare?

'Face the reality of how difficult it will be,' says Marshall Goldsmith, author of *Succession: Are You Ready?* 'Don't kid yourself that it's going to be easy. But remember it's not personal either – these are challenges anyone would face.'

If possible, Mr Goldsmith says, you should ask the incumbent before they leave to help you develop relationships with the key people as that will help smooth the transition.

Should I try to be like my predecessor?

No, according to Bill George, professor of management practice at Harvard Business School and a director of ExxonMobil and Goldman Sachs. He says: 'You should be yourself. Have the courage to make changes. An excellent example of someone who stepped into big shoes well was Sam Palmisano [who succeeded Lou Gerstner at IBM]. He re-established what IBM stood for.'

Another example, he adds, is Andrew Witty: 'He replaced Jean-Pierre Garnier at GlaxoSmithKline and he has done it his own way.' The trick, he says, 'is having a view of what your long-term impact is going to be'.

So how do I plough my own furrow?

Do a top-to-bottom reassessment of strategy. Ask if people are the right team for you and if they can shift their loyalties. 'If they can't, move them into retirement,' says Mr George. 'You can't have people pining for your predecessor.'

Ideally, you look for a mix of existing people and new blood, says Elisabeth Marx, a partner at Heidrick & Struggles, the recruitment company: 'You want to keep some core elements but set your own agenda and style.'

Today's fast-changing business environment makes this easier. Even a towering figure's modus operandi may be starting to look old-fashioned by the time they leave. In the oil industry, for instance, incoming chief executives are often happier now to talk about global warming. This is less a repudiation of the predecessor than an indication of which way the wind is blowing.

Will I be compared to my predecessor?

Of course you will: in some ways, the biggest challenge is your predecessor and not success in its own right. But you must resist the urge to compete with them and never, ever criticize them. 'Respect your predecessor's success,' says Mr Goldsmith. 'And if you're asked why you're doing things differently, talk about changing global conditions.'

Remember that direct comparisons can be nonsensical. Your predecessor may have had five years of a booming economy, while you take over at the start of a recession.

You may also discover that some great reputations aren't entirely justified, says Mr George. 'Chuck Prince took over from Sandy Weill who was viewed as a legend at Citigroup, and then spent his first year cleaning up the mess.' But even in these situations, you should take a leaf out of the American presidential handbook – never overtly badmouth the person before you, even if you have good reason to do so.

It sounds a thankless task; are there any upsides?

'I see it as a very positive scenario,' says Ms Marx. 'Although it is a double challenge, there are big pluses, too. You have a great role model and your team will be inspired and geared up. It should also give you confidence that a company that had this charismatic, high-impact leader has chosen you as a replacement.'

What's the biggest worry?

One thing to really beware of is a predecessor who's spending all their time playing golf. You don't want the spectre of their return hanging over you. Rather, you want to be in a position like Steven Ballmer. He may have plenty of challenges but as his predecessor is now focused on eradicating disease in Africa, the possibility of Bill Gate's return to Microsoft is not one of them.

Boosting your ambition

Ambition is an oddity in the workplace toolkit. It varies across cultures and organizations, with some people finding it distasteful while for others it is the single most important factor in shaping their career. Given that it can sometimes make the difference between success and failure, is it possible to take steps to boost it?

Can I turn myself into a serial entrepreneur or CEO of a dozen companies?

Probably not, says Cary Cooper, professor of organizational psychology at Lancaster University. 'Really driven people like entrepreneurs who keep doing it again and again usually have a drive that comes from something traumatic in their childhood. However, he says, for most people not having this is a good thing. 'No matter how successful [driven people] are, they'll never quite believe it and they'll never be satisfied – their success doesn't make them happy; they just keep going.'

What about cultivating a more healthy ambition?

Instead of looking at obsessives who are working themselves into the ground, you are better off taking your cues from people who seem to enjoy what they are doing and appear genuinely enthused by it. These people tend to stick with one thing or in one area and their good fortune is usually a mixture of interest and hard work.

So how do I boost my ambition?

'The key to ambition is understanding your motivations – if you can understand these, that makes sense of everything else,' says Corinne Mills of Personal Career Management. 'I was talking to a banker the other day who said he was motivated by money. But actually when we dug around a bit, we discovered he was really motivated by security.' Similarly, she adds, people who believe they have to take the next obvious job up are often temperamentally ill-suited for it. 'When people feel as if they're stuck, it's often because they're looking for the wrong thing.'

There are two other very important ways to boost your drive: 'You need to start to take risks,' says Ms Mills. 'Ambitious people do not just sit in the same job. Apply for new positions, network, and really get yourself out of your comfort zone.' Risk-taking is something that virtually all ambitious people do far better than also-rans. Finally, you should not make excuses: rather than moaning about your lot, you need to look at whatever it is you are doing and do the best you possibly can. For example, if you wait for the perfect role for your talents, you will wait forever.

Is ambition all about money and power?

John Drysdale, managing director of Momentum Executive Development, says he is witnessing a shift in the way people view ambition. 'Of course people still work hard, but they're seeing ambition less in terms of just money and power. You want to get to the top, but you want people to respect you too. I think the paradigm is shifting – particularly as we're currently looking at the consequences of too much uncritical ambition.'

Is an extra dose of ambition all I need to revitalize my career?

No. While talent without ambition can be cute, ambition without talent results in the kind of tragi-comic mini-megalomaniacs you see booted out of *The Apprentice* in early rounds. It is probably best to think of it as a catalyst that makes your other attributes perform better – but the raw material needs to be there first.

How to be a leader

A mistake executives often make is thinking that being a leader and being a manager are the same thing. But while there are similarities, the two are quite distinct.

What is the difference between managing and leading?

There is often a great deal of overlap and most management roles do have a leadership element; the trick is to combine the two successfully. However, the higher you climb, the greater the leadership element gets.

Jane Clarke of Nicholson McBride, the business psychologists, says that many people fail to understand this relationship. 'Management tends to be quite hands-on, while leaders need to reach a wider group and articulate a vision and strategy. A lot of it is bigger-picture stuff rather than doing more of what made you a successful manager.'

In fact, where many leaders go wrong is that they spend too much time managing. 'Management is ensuring everyone gets their budgets done on time. Leadership is raising everyone's performance by 5 per cent,' says Helen Pitcher, chairman of IDDAS, a boardroom effectiveness consultancy.

Is there a template for leadership?

The only model is to be authentic, explains Ms Pitcher. 'You need to be clear about what you are as a person and what your values are,' she says.

When many people replace successful leaders, they often try to be like the person they have replaced. 'But research shows there are thousands of leadership traits, so there is no one right kind of leader,' she adds.

Is leadership just high-level stuff?

'You need to stay up on the balcony where you can see what's happening on the dance floor, rather than being on the dance floor,' says Virginia Merritt, a partner at Stanton Marris, a strategy consultancy.

Leading also has a far stronger political element than managing. However, she adds: 'You need to deal with the emotional stuff as well. You have to tune into the mood of people and connect with them. Leaders are influencers and persuaders. It's a fine balancing act.'

Here, says Ms Clarke, 'a little self-disclosure can be very helpful. You need to have gravitas and presence, but you need to talk about your feelings.'

What unpleasant duties does a leader have?

'You must be able to give tough love,' says Ms Pitcher. 'Be prepared to have those conversations. As a leader you get the behaviour you accept. If one of your team is underperforming, what are you doing that allows them to get away with that?'

Ms Clarke adds that leading in difficult times can mean making a lot of hard decisions. 'When times are good you may be able to fund two proposals, both of which have merits. Now, you are far more likely to have to choose.'

What about leadership teams?

The temptation, says Ms Clarke, 'is to recruit in your own image and you should avoid that'.

Ms Merritt adds: 'You need to surround yourself with the right people, including people who will tell you you're wrong and people who may be better than you in some areas. It's very easy to get in a bubble.'

Leaders are also likely to have strong, deep networks that allow them to exert influence informally.

Are some people not cut out for leadership?

Many people who believe they're not cut out for leadership are actually not cut out for their perception of leadership. 'Rather than being a charismatic, highly visible leader, you might be a quiet leader,' says Ms Pitcher. It's also worth remembering that there are other forms of leadership – such as thought leadership – which allow you to exert considerable influence without being at the very top of the tree. But leadership is difficult and demanding even when times are good – and it really isn't for everyone.

Being important and being liked

We're always being told that leaders should be respected and trusted. But should they be liked too? And, if so, how do you convince your staff that you're a nice person?

Is being popular good for my career?

It is not a prerequisite, but it will make your working life easier. 'I'd argue that all good bosses should be trusted and respected, but some of them go beyond that and are actually liked,' says social entrepreneur Jo Owen. To be liked, 'you need to genuinely care about people and their careers. People who do this tend to be rated very highly and inspire great loyalty.'

Arabella Ellis at leadership consultancy Thinking Partnership says: 'A big part of leadership is getting people to go the extra mile and being liked will help you do that. But it's a bit like being a parent – your goal should be to create an atmosphere of respect and trust, not to be everyone's best friend.'

How do I stay liked on the way up?

'In some ways it's hardest to be liked in middle management because your colleagues are also your competitors,' says Mr Owen.

Ceri Roderick of business psychologists Pearn Kandola adds that it is possible to be competitive without being nasty. 'You can actually get away with being unpleasant to people on your way up, because you get promoted away from them quite quickly, but sooner or later it usually comes back to bite you,' he says.

'It's also a reputational thing. If you are unpleasant or insincere to people, they will tell other people and a bad reputation is very hard to change.'

Mr Roderick says that as you move higher in a company, people skills become more, not less, important as your results are more likely to depend on the work of others.

What can I do to connect to those who work for me?

At higher levels, Mr Owen says, 'you need to get out of the C-suite and talk and listen to ordinary people. It's not about doing factory inspections with line managers, it's about conversations with people. It's about having cups of tea. It's not complicated but it does take courage.'

It is also better to spend 10 minutes with one person than it is to spend 10 seconds with 30 people. Talk – and, just as importantly, listen – to a few people and they'll tell others about it. 'Once you've spoken to a number of people you leverage the gossip network. Do it well and your reputation can spread like wildfire.'

Are there any other traits that help?

Ms Ellis says humour is a great way of building bridges with staff. 'Being able to laugh – especially at yourself – does a great deal to humanize you. You should also have a little humility about you too. Don't believe you're a leader because you're better; acknowledge the role of chance. Stay grounded – this can be a real challenge as the higher you get, the less you're criticized. Listen to friends, spouses and kids – people who won't tell you just what they think you want to hear.'

Are there any downsides to being liked?

The obvious drawback is that people who want to be liked too much will be thought weak. 'Those who are naturally too agreeable put relationships ahead of getting things done,' says Mr Roderick. 'You have to work on the right level of agreeableness.'

Taking more risks

An appetite for risk can help differentiate business superstars from also-rans. But there is a fine line between being bold and being fool-hardy. So how do you take smart risks?

Why take risks at all?

'You have to ask yourself, "Do I want to work in a role or organization where there's very little chance anything will go wrong or do I want to put myself in a riskier position where there are potentially far greater rewards?"' says Ian Gooden, chief operating officer of Chiumento, a human resources consultancy. 'Putting yourself at risk is the price you pay to climb the next rung of the corporate ladder.'

Risks are not just big moves. Rather, you should be taking smaller risks continually. 'You need to keep taking measured risks all the time,' says Peter Shaw, an executive coach at Praesta. 'They expand your repertoire and extend your capabilities.'

Alma Erlich, a psychologist who is head of change at the MBS recruitment group, points out that 'You take risks even if you don't take risks because the world around you changes.'

How should I approach risks?

You need to look at them in a holistic way. 'Look at the upsides,' says Mr Shaw. 'Ask yourself what would bring you joy. That will help you think about risk in a less scary way. Then ask yourself about the downsides.'

Be self-aware and contextualize risk. 'If you take big risks in one area, you might be comparatively risk free in others,' explains Mr Shaw. 'People who take what appear to be crazy risks are often much more sensible than they might appear. Think of your life as a kind of investment portfolio of risk.' However, he explains, while you need to view risks coolly and objectively, you shouldn't entirely let your head rule, 'You can analyse things to death, so you should listen to your heart too.'

What if I don't take enough risks?

If you find that you have become very risk averse in your career, Mr Shaw suggests taking risks in other areas of your life where you are more comfortable doing so. 'If you run every day, run five miles instead of three,' he says. 'Push yourself and think about how these risks can translate back into your career. Also think about times that you've taken risks in the past and they've worked. Imagine yourself taking the risk [in question] and what the potential benefits might be.'

What should I avoid?

'A bad risk is where you put yourself in a position where your goals aren't clear,' says Mr Gooden. 'You need to know that success is measurable and defined.'

Ms Elrich says you need to avoid the gambler's trap: 'You shouldn't get into a position where you automatically think of yourself as a winner. Don't become immune to the downside of risk.'

Do not underestimate the power of an organization's culture, either. 'Leaders need to ensure that those under them are taking the right amount of risk,' says Ms Erlich – noting that sometimes, in businesses such as Enron and some investment banks before the bust, risk-taking had become too celebrated. 'Sometimes greed and bravado become praiseworthy and sensible voices get shouted down.'

What if things go wrong?

'If you get it wrong, hold up your hands and acknowledge it,' says Mr Gooden. 'Say you made the wrong choice.' It is also worth talking to people who have tried and failed, and remember: many new careers rise from the ashes of old ones.

How to prioritize

Along with information overload, many managers also suffer from to-do list overload, with dozens of tasks vying for their attention. How do you make sure you tackle the ones that really matter?

Planning is the first step

'Prioritization comes down to planning,' says Clare Evans, a time management coach. 'Write down what it is you want to do and work out where these things fit into your overall goals.'

Ben Williams, a corporate psychologist, advises dividing tasks into achievable targets. 'If you have a goal like, "I want to open up a new market," break it down into objectives that are very specific and measurable and give yourself a target date for the objectives.'

You must then look at day-to-day tasks and determine if they advance you towards the objective. It is, he explains, 'about establishing where you get the most benefit'.

He also suggests writing down lists the night before, as 'your unconscious solves problems when you're asleep'.

What if I'm still unsure?

In large organizations – and particularly if you have multiple bosses – it can still be extra difficult to identify priorities. If you're unsure, ask your customers, line managers and colleagues what they consider important. If you have a mentor, ask them.

Geraldine Gallacher, an executive coach, says: 'You need to know what you're good at. Think about where you stand out. What are you known for?'

She adds that unimportant tasks should be delegated. 'You should have a not-to-do list – and you need to be quite ruthless.'

What about other people's priorities?

Ms Gallacher says that this is not easy. 'You can often question or challenge the person. Is this important for me to do? Is this a priority? Or you can say no. Explain that you already have things to do. Ask them, "Which task do you want me to do?"' Obviously the degree of push-back will depend on a variety of factors and there is a political element – unimportant tasks can become important if they are for important people.

Where do people go wrong?

Lack of planning is the biggest problem, says Ms Evans. 'People often aren't clear what their goals are. You need to look at everything. No one has time to do it all, but if you don't plan, you won't know what's important.' Assuming you have planned you must still stick to what is important: most people rightly tackle tasks that are urgent and important first. But many then make the mistake of moving on to tasks that are urgent, but not important. 'Successful people stay in the important area,' says Ms Gallacher.

Mr Williams cautions: 'You need to watch out for time predators – people who say, "Can you just do that for me?"'

And it's not just people: sitting in front of a PC, it's very easy to let e-mail dictate the order in which you do things.

Again, it all comes back to having clear goals: if you don't have a plan, you quickly become part of someone else's. This said, while you should plan, you shouldn't map out every single minute of your day. 'Build in a bit of slack so if something goes wrong, it doesn't throw everything out,' says Ms Evans.

What about priorities outside work?

'Many people have incredibly full-on careers, and they give other areas like health and fitness and recreation and socializing very low priorities,' says Ms Gallacher. This is a mistake as these things provide balance, reduce stress and are likely to improve your performance. 'You should diary things like going to the gym and meeting friends. They are important.'

Having the right attitude

We are often told that having the right attitude is incredibly important in any job. But what is the right attitude – and how can you develop it? And what do you do if others have the wrong one?

What is the right attitude?

There are two parts to having a good attitude at work. One is organization specific, the other more general. Arabella Ellis of leadership consultancy the Thinking Partnership says you need to identify the former: 'Many people make the mistake of believing they start with the right attitude and don't check that their idea of the right attitude is also their organization's. If you don't have the right attitude for your company, you'll work very hard and get nowhere.'

Nonetheless, she stresses the importance of retaining your authenticity and fitting into a culture without losing yourself: 'There's a balance between being compliant and being defiant.'

Changes such as a new boss can mean changes in what the right attitude is.

As for your more general attitude in the workplace, Peter Shaw, author of *Living Leadership*, says it all comes down to your outlook. 'You choose your attitude. We make a choice every day. Will we be a victim or grouchy; will we see opportunities and focus on doing things better?'

How can I develop a better attitude?

'Be positive and creative,' says corporate psychologist Ben Williams. 'Try and have fun and look for the good in situations. Do nice things and compliment people. You should also be focused on the moment. If you're with someone, be with them, not on your phone or on the computer. Accept full responsibility for the choices you make. People enjoy jobs more when they get into them, so you need to commit to what you're doing.'

Ms Ellis adds: 'Try and understand other people and business goals and what they stand for. Spend time negotiating expectations so you can deliver in your own way.' She adds that you also need political intelligence and that you should know – and acknowledge – your own strengths and weaknesses.

Look too at those around you whose attitudes work – what is it that they do that you could be doing? Mr Shaw says, 'Recognize you can see things in more than one way. There's a lot to be said for an open mind.'

What if my team or colleagues have a bad attitude?

'You can change your workplace,' says Mr Williams. 'If the attitude is bad, praise people and be nice, acknowledge people. You'll become an oasis. It's like a cold bed – the warmth will spread.'

Mr Shaw adds: 'Attitude is infectious and you can infect others with a good or bad attitude. Time is finite. But energy you can create. There isn't a fixed amount of goodwill.'

However, he adds that you must be realistic: 'If someone's very negative you may want to give yourself a bit of distance so it doesn't drag you down. You could talk about it and think about why they feel negative. If this goes on for a long time you might need to talk about it to your boss.'

How do I affect the attitude of my employees?

'One of a manager's key responsibilities is how they affect a team's attitude and how they enable people to have a positive attitude,' says Mr Shaw. 'Some people just need a little encouragement. Others need strong performance management and steering.'

'If you have to criticize people,' says Mr Williams, 'criticize the behaviour, not the individual – and find something good to say too. End on a compliment.'

The goal, says Mr Shaw, should be creating a workplace 'that is both positive and focused on results'.

Commanding respect

Being respected is a big part of being a successful manager. But how do you gain the respect of your colleagues?

Is there a template for being respected?

The best way to start is to be the better part of who you are. 'You have to be authentic,' says Gareth Jones, a visiting professor at IE Business School in Madrid. 'People expect consistency across words and deeds. If they spot a gap between what you say and what you do then you've had it as a leader.'

You should also be comfortable with where you come from. 'When a lot of people become successful, they try to acquire a different kind of cultural capital and appear something they're not. You can change your future but not your past – and trying to do this will make you look like a bit of a fraud.'

Do I have to be liked?

'A lot of people still confuse being liked with being respected,' says David Pendleton, a founder of Edgecumbe Group, the organizational psychologists. 'But it is much more important to be trusted. Respect and trust are pretty interchangeable. It's important not to be disliked but if you are consistent, you can be respected without being liked.'

What other attributes are useful?

It is difficult to respect the incompetent. 'Being good at something helps to demonstrate your legitimacy,' says Professor Jones. 'In a knowledge business, you are likely to have very clever people working for you so what you're good at might be winning resources for those people.'

Mr Pendleton adds that you should also 'have something interesting and insightful to say about your marketplace. Understand how things work and take an active interest. But don't be a know it all.' But being competent and knowledgeable is not enough, though: people need to be able to rely on you. 'Follow through on your promises,' says Mr Pendleton. 'A lot of people overcommit and under-deliver. It is far better to do the reverse.'

What about my relationships with others?

'It might seem obvious, but follow the golden rule and treat others as you would like to be treated,' says Michael Crom, chief learning officer at Dale Carnegie Training. 'If you treat others with respect, they will respect you. Be genuinely interested in the people you work with and make an effort to get to know them.'

He adds that you should help others in their careers. 'Inspire people and remove barriers to their success. If you help them to succeed, they'll want you to succeed. You'll be propelled up the ladder.'

But, says Mr Pendleton, sometimes you will need the courage to take unpopular positions: 'If these are consistent with who you are, people will respect you for it.'

What if I feel insufficiently respected?

'There is no easy, direct line to it. Changing poor perceptions takes time and repetition,' says Mr Pendleton.

However, there are people who are naturally disrespectful. 'Don't be thin-skinned and fragile,' he adds. 'But if it is a real issue, tackle it head on.'

Being more confident

Confidence can make or break your career. Luckily for those lacking it, self-belief is easy to boost and easy to create – and the more confident you are the more confident you become.

How important is confidence?

'Hugely from a leadership and team perspective,' says Rob Yeung, a corporate psychologist at Talentspace and author of *Confidence: The Art of Getting Whatever You Want.*

'You must be confident for others to have confidence in you. People equate confidence with competence.'

Bob Etherington, a sales, negotiation and presentation trainer, says it can be the difference between success and failure. 'Companies aren't run by people who are the best but by people who think they're the best.'

Is confidence innate?

'Some of it is,' says Mr Yeung, 'It's a personality trait – a mixture of genes and upbringing. But you can push it up a couple of points.' You can do this by having the right attitude and telling yourself you can do something. This plus practice will result in greater confidence. Very few people are truly confident and comfortable the first time they speak publicly, but they usually are by the tenth.

What about faking it?

'Often you do need to feign confidence at first,' says Mr Etherington. 'You try and adopt the feeling of someone who knows what they're doing.'

But, he adds, the best thing about faking confidence is that it often evolves into the real thing. 'You get a picture in your mind of the outcome you want. Athletes do it all the time – they see the ball going into the hole. Even though you don't really believe it, your brain latches on to it. That gets your confidence going.'

Peter Shaw, an executive coach at Praesta, says, 'Confidence is a self-fulfilling prophecy – if you seem confident people will believe in you and you'll be more confident.'

What can I do to build my confidence?

When engaging in conversation or making presentations, Mr Etherington's advice is: 'Speak clearly and drop your voice, stand with your feet about 30 centimetres apart, use your hands when you talk and make eye contact.'

Mr Shaw says that personal experiences can also help. 'Remember occasions when you have been confident in the past. Encapsulate memories of success,' he says. 'You could also have a mantra, like "I can do this" or "Keep calm and carry on." Or you can think of situations where you're confident outside work and then transfer some of that into the work environment.'

Mr Yeung says: 'Psychologists also talk about the "illusion of transparency". Most people believe that when they are nervous everyone can see this. But they can't. Just remembering this can make you more confident.'

How important is preparation?

Two ways to improve how you come across are to make sure you have done your homework and to show up to meetings with plenty of time to spare. 'You may not actually need to read all those pages the night before but it will boost your confidence,' says Mr Shaw. 'Preparation is as much psychological as practical.'

Arriving early is also a good way to collect your thoughts. 'If you arrive flustered and have to apologize, you won't inspire confidence in those you're meeting and you start on the back foot.'

Can you be overconfident?

There is a fine line between self-belief and arrogance. A confident manager is grounded enough to 'accept criticism and welcome feedback', says Mr Yeung.

Chapter Eleven
The stuff nobody likes at work

Workplace fights

Tougher, tenser times have made for more conflict in the office. But can you avoid workplace spats? If not, how do you manage them? And are there some fights that are worth fighting?

Should I avoid all conflict?

Having regular office rows does little for your reputation but conflict is part of human nature and the idea of teams working in perfect alignment is fallacious. You might agree on a lot of things but there are plenty of areas where heated disagreement is an important driver of success and innovation.

'There are times when it's better to get things out in the open,' says Jane Bird, director of good practice services at Acas. 'It's often a very good thing to find the courage to tell someone that you don't like the way things are.'

But it has to be productive dissent – anyone can pick a fight.

Are there times when I should instigate conflict?

When deciding whether a point of view is worth fighting for, Saj-Nicole Joni, co-author of *The Right Fight*, says the questions you should ask yourself are: 'Does it really matter? Is it about the future rather than settling old scores?' and 'Is it for a noble purpose?' She notes that a few more 'right fights' within banks in the mid-2000s could have been a very good thing.

Gillian Ku, associate professor of organizational psychology at London Business School, says: 'You might also use strategic displays of anger to help you get more stuff. These are usually when the other party doesn't have a lot of leverage.'

What if conflict is unavoidable or the fight finds me?

'Conduct yourself in a high-minded way,' says Ms Joni. 'Think sport not war and ideas not personalities. Be attuned to networks to ensure you don't cause unintended consequences. And honour the person who doesn't win.'

Interestingly, Ms Joni adds, one reason we are seeing more conflict is because cash-strapped companies can no longer make problems go away by funding two different points of view.

If the fight comes to you (perhaps in the form of an angry person), Professor Ku says you should break the cycle of escalation. 'Step back, take a second, apologize (sometimes worth doing even if it's not your fault) or bring in a neutral third party.'

What if the fight is not mine?

If a heated dispute erupts in your patch, a judgement needs to be made – raised voices are one thing, fisticuffs at the water cooler are another. 'Some fights are no big deal,' advises Ms Bird, 'People will raise their voices, but they'll be friends at the pub that evening.' If things are more serious, take the individuals aside and try to talk to them separately. There is no reason why people who have been shouting at each other should not continue to work together, especially if their manager helps them address the root causes. 'A good manager who can deal with these situations in a sensitive manner is worth their weight in gold,' says Ms Bird.

What if things get nasty?

Most companies have rules to deal with situations that escalate beyond what might be termed a constructive dispute, although if things get that far, well-meant policies are usually 'wallpaper' for what takes place in the heat of the moment.

'The first thing to do is stop the violence and calm things down,' says Professor Ku. After that, it could be anything from an apology and a quiet word all the way to a more formal approach with a dispute resolution service, although this really should be a last resort.

Bouncing back from failure

The difficult business climate of the past few years has meant that blunders that might once have been brushed aside can now result in censure or worse. So how do you bounce back from a career low? And can you emerge with your reputation enhanced?

Are there different types of career disaster?

'You need to differentiate between a corporate failure and personal failure,' says Cary Cooper, professor of organizational psychology at Lancaster University. If the disaster is caused by events beyond your control, then it is much easier to deal with and you may have plenty of company. If the buck stops with you, rather less so.

He adds that there is also a lesser category of failure where you make a 'career-limiting move' that doesn't result in your losing your job but irreparably damages your professional standing.

What should I do first?

'If you're accused of bullying or plagiarism or demoted – something you can't live down – it's probably best to stay in your role a while and then look for another job where you won't be identified with the problem,' says Professor Cooper.

If your career appears to be in tatters, you need to face up to it, mourn and move on as quickly as possible.

Don't wallow in misery, advises Gerald Ratner, the jewellery retailer who left the business that carried his family name when he described one of its products as 'total crap'.

'It took me seven years to come back,' he says. 'I just gave up. I was lying in bed watching *Countdown* and my wife said, "You can't go on like this." I should have put my hands up immediately and said, "I screwed up very badly and made a horrendous mistake," rather than moping around like a wounded soldier feeling sorry for myself.'

Mr Ratner adds: 'The worst thing to do is start taking anti-depressants; they turn you into a zombie and you can't network or start to rebuild your life. Do something that clears your head like taking long bike rides.'

How do I rebuild my career?

This is what your network and your contacts are there for. Of course, you will be damaged goods for a while, but if you show the appropriate level of contrition and remorse, many will forgive you and help you get on with the process of reinventing yourself.

You may have to take a step down, try something completely new or start at the beginning again. Donald Trump once told *Fortune* magazine that, while heavily indebted in the early 1990s, he saw a beggar and thought: 'That bum isn't worth a dime but at least he's at zero… That puts him $900 million ahead of me.'

Jonathan Aitken, the disgraced Tory MP, became active in prison reform after his career disaster. And in a more moderate vein many of those whose fortunes crashed with the financial sector have retrained in areas perceived as more socially useful such as teaching. For his part, says Mr Ratner, 'When I finally pulled myself together, I went out and opened a health club which I sold three years later for £3.9 million.'

Above all, says Professor Cooper, you must get back on the treadmill. Moreover, as business is a very competitive and often unsympathetic environment, you may find that once you start to fight back people are much more willing to help you than they were when you were at your lowest ebb.

Can I turn a negative into a positive?

For many entrepreneurs, career setbacks are almost expected and form an entertaining part of a swashbuckling CV. Mr Ratner says that when he launched Gerald Online, a jewellery website, initial interest was very much down to his notoriety – 'although you do get a bit tired of being a poster boy for failure for something you said 19 years ago'. That said, some mistakes (such as those which lead to deaths or the defrauding of vulnerable people) can be rather harder to live down and leave a nastier taste.

How do I find the right frame of mind?

'Accept that setbacks will happen and that everyone has bad luck and lapses of judgement,' says Mr Ratner. 'You need a sense of humour about these things. OK, I lost a £500 million business, but nobody died. I've learnt to laugh about it.'

How to take criticism

Nobody likes to be criticized. But being able to deal with criticism well can make you look stronger, more confident and mature. So how do you find the upside of a dressing down?

How should you react initially?

Stay cool. 'We have an embedded reaction which is to go on the defensive and argue,' says Jon Cowell, an associate consultant at business psychologists Edgecumbe. 'But you shouldn't give in to this. Instead seek clarification. Say things like why do you feel this way and could you give me an example. This can help you to understand the criticism, but even if you're just buying time until the emotional response dies down it's a good idea.'

Graham Abbey, an executive coach at March Friday, says: 'If you disagree with the criticism you might use phrases like "That surprises me and I need to go away and think about it."' As well as giving you a bit of distance, it also shows you don't implicitly accept it.

If you are being criticized publicly, you should try and move it to somewhere more private.

How do you analyse criticism?

'There's always context,' says Mr Abbey. 'The key question is "What's the intention behind it?" People give feedback for reasons other than help – it might be to cut you down or get you back. Understanding this alters the nature of how you take it and the weight you give it. Ask what's in it for them. You can always learn from feedback, although it may not be what the giver intends. You need to look at the message and the messenger.'

That said, you also need to be objective about yourself and remember that some criticism can be very useful.

How do you respond more thoughtfully?

'Research shows there are two strategies that work well,' says Mr Cowell. 'The first is collaboration and the second is confrontation. So engage your critics or disagree. But don't avoid it, divert attention or personalize it.'

If you need to rebut criticism, says Mr Abbey, the received wisdom is to stick to facts and examples – although this can be easier said than done. 'You might explain where you're coming from coolly, rationally and from a distance.'

If the criticism is fair, acknowledge that you are in the wrong and if it is insightful, say so and show a willingness to learn. Perhaps the best thing you can do, though, is to make your critic part of the solution.

'Getting people involved in the solution is a powerful way of bringing them onside,' says Mr Cowell. 'It also makes it harder for them to criticize your response to their criticism.'

Can I ignore some criticism?

You shouldn't really ignore criticism entirely. But, says Mr Cowell, 'If people are serial critics who are riding their hobby horses, acknowledge them and move on.' You might also want to acknowledge the legitimacy of some criticism while making it clear to the person that you will not be following their suggested course of action.'

·Does it make a difference if I'm a manager?

'Teams that don't work are often teams where the leader is distant and people don't feel they can criticize them,' says Mr Cowell. In fact, managers should thank those who give them good critical feedback and help them to do so.

Mr Abbey says: 'The worst scenario is getting no criticism at all. You wind up very cut off and this is a risk as you move higher, as it can be very hard for criticism to flow upwards. Never being criticized often results in spectacular disasters in the longer run.' Of course, it's worth remembering that an overly critical environment can be destructive too.

How do I know that it has been dealt with to the satisfaction of all concerned?

'It is definitely worth going back to people,' says David Ferrabee, managing director of Able and How, change communications consultants. 'You never know if you've solved the problem until you have outside validation. As a manager this is especially important.'

Overbearing colleagues

Loud, domineering co-workers can drown out quietly effective ones. Worse, their high profile often means they get noticed and promoted. So how can you ensure that your voice gets heard? And can you use overbearing colleagues to your advantage?

Where should I start?

'Begin by being objective about yourself,' says Corinne Mills of Personal Career Management. 'You need to be careful about what you see as overbearing. They might just be getting attention because they're really good at their job or have an excellent communication style. You could be jealous.'

Therefore ask your colleagues to see if your view is shared.

You should also look at the culture you are in, says Robert Sutton, professor of management science and engineering at Stanford University. 'Sales team-type cultures often reward people who are loud and overbearing.' If this is the case, there may not be much you can do about it.

Finally, don't worry too much about people who are nothing but noise: they rarely last long. It is the ones who are reasonably good and overbearing who are the problem.

What about practical tips for dealing with the issue?

'When the person walks into your space, stand up,' says Ceri Roderick, emeritus partner at business psychologists Pearn Kandola. 'It shows you're happy to talk for two minutes but not that you're about to relax. In meetings you can ask thoughtful questions that cause people to stop and think, like "How will this look to the market?" These slow people down.'

Ms Mills adds: 'You might agree an agenda for the meeting. Say "You do this bit and I'll cover that bit" – but make sure you go first.'

Professor Sutton says: 'Sometimes you have to be sneaky. If it's just a short-term project, don't invite the overbearing person to the meeting.'

Can I approach them?

'Those who are overbearing and extrovert are often lacking in self-awareness,' says Professor Sutton. 'They may be oblivious.' Sometimes just talking to them can help.

'Point it out,' says Mr Roderick. 'Help them to develop some empathy. Bear in mind they could be feeling anxious too. If you're quiet and feel awkward being in the spotlight, remember that extroverts feel awkward being out of it. But make it about the behaviour, not the individual.'

Professor Sutton says that sometimes there may safety in numbers. 'You may not wish to take them out yourself. Build up a posse for self-protection. One useful thing you can say is "You're not seen as a good team player."'

How do I ensure my own achievements are noticed?

'Be sensible about the visibility of what you do,' says Mr Roderick. 'Don't hide your good works away in a corner.'

Ms Mills says that if a colleague's overbearing ways do result in them getting attention or promotion, 'Don't slag them off to your boss. It just looks like envy. Rather what you need to do is work on having a good relationship with your manager and the decision makers. So even if they are grandstanding, you have the back channels.'

Is there any way of using the overbearing colleague to your advantage?

'Sometimes the correct thing to do is to recognize that one person is the politician and the loudmouth and the other is the doer,' says Professor Sutton. 'So you form a coalition, where you provide the substance and the overbearing person gives you credit and sells you.'

What if it's my boss?

A boss who likes the sound of their own voice is a very difficult thing as all you can really do is steer them. Ms Mills suggests going into meetings with them, armed with excuses. 'Say you have another meeting or a phone call and tell them before the meeting starts.'

If you are a manager, says Mr Roderick, you need to ensure everyone has a chance to speak: 'A good manager will hear the quietest voice in the room.'

Working for a struggling company

Working for a business that is going through a rough patch is always a challenge. But it can have a surprising number of upsides and opportunities as long as you look after your own interests.

Where's the bright side?

'People in adversity are often actually quite galvanized,' says executive coach Geraldine Gallacher. 'A burning platform provides a clear common goal for the team and so, ironically, they pull together well.'

'It's good to get some perspective,' says Miranda Kennett of First Class Coach. 'Try and find some things that are good about the organization and places where you can make a difference.'

It is also worth noting that when the difficult times end, the upturn can be very sudden and those who have stayed the course are usually well placed to reap the rewards.

How do I make the most of it?

'You can often pick up a huge breadth of experience,' says Clive Davis, director of the financial recruiter, Robert Half. 'Those who are prepared to make the best of things will see an increased demand for their skills. You'll get access to work and responsibilities you probably wouldn't get normally, although you may find yourself doing one-and-a-half jobs.'

Ms Kennett adds: 'Promotion can be very rapid – there are often big opportunities as senior people may leave and not be replaced.'

For all this, you also need to have one eye on opportunities elsewhere. 'Ensure your network is active, and stay in contact with a good recruiter,' says Mr Davis.

What do I watch out for?

'Loyalty is a really good thing up to a point,' says Ms Kennett. 'But you need to remember that individuals will always be more loyal to a business than the business will be to them. You need to look after your best interests and, if necessary, devise an exit plan.'

Ms Gallacher says people often slip into reactive, firefighting behaviours: 'Strategizing in difficult circumstances is essential but all too often the urgent supersedes the important.'

She adds that managers should be aware of how their behaviour looks: 'Leaders need to be very conscious of the signals they are sending out as people are hyper-vigilant in tough times.'

How do I ensure that my accomplishments are recognized?

'Document your successes and keep track of improvements,' says Ms Gallacher.

Mr Davis agrees: 'Get recognized, get extra responsibility and build up a dossier that shows where you have boosted company performance.'

How do I play it if I get an interview elsewhere?

'Say to another employer: "This is what I learnt. I have the benefit of this experience,"' says Mr Davis. 'Promote yourself as someone who can handle themselves when the going gets tough. Make sure you have a story to tell in that regard.'

Ms Gallacher adds: 'Potential employers will be interested in how you deal with adversity. Personal resilience is reckoned to be one of the key leadership attributes of the future.'

However, Ms Kennett cautions against badmouthing your current company. 'The last thing you want to do is be critical of your employer. And if you're feeling bitter, you're not in the right place to be doing interviews.' However, she says, 'You should try and distance yourself from the negatives, especially anything like dishonesty or incompetence. Obviously, the more senior you are, the more difficult it can be.'

Handling favouritism

Favouritism in the office can be frustrating and demotivating. But it can also be difficult to prove. How do you determine whether it is actually occurring and, if so, what can you do about it?

Are you sure it is favouritism?

'A lot of perceived favouritism may not actually be favouritism,' says Owen Morgan, a director at HR consultancy Penna. 'It's hard to identify and can be quite subtle.'

Blaire Palmer, managing director of executive coaching organization Taming Tigers, says that often you and your manager just won't be a good match. 'If you aren't being favoured today, chances are you may have been in the past,' she says. 'It's just not your moment. Sometimes you'll have just made the wrong assumptions about what your manager is looking for. Or you just don't know them well enough.'

Mr Morgan says, 'It is always worth checking with your colleagues. It might be just that the "favoured" person has a better relationship with their boss than you do for any number of reasons. Remember too that you may not be flagging up your presence.'

What can I do if it's minor favouritism?

'You need to be very professional about it,' says Ms Palmer. 'Ask your manager what he or she is looking for. Make an effort to understand them. Not so you can pretzel yourself into different shapes to please them but so you know what they want.'

As Jane Clarke of business psychologists Nicholson McBride says, you can't really barge in and ask: 'Why X?' But you can have a discussion about what really works.

'Your boss may not even realize they're doing it,' says Mr Morgan. 'Then it's a very straightforward conversation. Say: "It always seems like Bill gets those projects. Could I do some?"'

Finally, Ms Palmer says you shouldn't be too thin-skinned. 'Ask yourself why it matters. If it's just annoying and seems a bit unfair, then the best thing may be to learn to live with it. The workplace can be quite rough and tumble. We expect organizations to be like a family but they're often more like the playground.'

What if it's more serious?

'If it's very overt, it can be easier to identify but harder to deal with,' says Mr Morgan. You need to remain constructive and even if the whole team agrees, you shouldn't get a posse of colleagues together and back your manager into a corner. 'Speak to HR – say you feel sidelined,' he says. 'Do it without pointing fingers. HR are quite attuned to this kind of thing and this can be a good place to raise it.'

Ms Clarke notes that favouritism is endemic in some companies. 'You see organizations where the whole thing operates on favouritism from the CEO down,' she says. If this is the case, it might be best to find another job.

Ms Palmer says that full-on whistle-blowing should be a last resort as even if you win, it is often a pyrrhic victory.

What if I am the favourite?

'Use your influence to help other members of the team,' says Ms Clarke. 'Flag up the contributions of others – you can afford to be generous and magnanimous.'

However, bear in mind that it is not unknown for managers to appear to favour people because they get on well personally and then promote someone else because their work is better. 'Don't take things for granted,' she advises. 'Spread your network and build good relationships with people other than your manager. Make sure you have support elsewhere.'

How to disagree with your boss

Sometimes you are going to disagree strongly with your line manager. But how do you do it in a way that minimizes conflict and unpleasantries, while ensuring that your point is made?

How should I tackle disagreement?

'Just saying "I don't think that is a good idea" doesn't work very well,' says Alan Redman, a business psychologist at Criterion Partnership. 'It's the wrong kind of approach. The first thing to do is to find agreement wherever you can. Before you tell your boss what you really think, tell them what it is that you like about their idea. You might have to be quite creative, but you're laying groundwork that makes you look reasonable.'

Mr Redman adds that language can help too. 'Don't use the word "but" as it signals disagreement; use "and" instead.'

Sandi Mann, author of *Managing Your Boss in a Week*, acknowledges that disagreeing is difficult: 'People naturally want to acquiesce and people like those who agree with them. Don't be confrontational, be assertive and steer them in the right direction.'

How do I suggest other ideas?

'You need to offer alternatives and show that you're trying to be helpful, not just obstreperous,' says executive coach Miranda Kennett.

But you need to be careful how you do it. The trick, says Mr Redman, is to 'present your ideas as alternatives rather than competing ideas'.

It may also help your case if you are not overly proprietorial about your suggestions; no one likes to think that their idea lost and somebody else's won. 'You have to use arguments that appeal to your boss,' Mr Redman says. 'Don't try to convince them with brute force of rational argument. Get at what's getting them to make the decision. Address the anxiety. Put yourself in their shoes.'

Ms Mann adds: 'The best thing to do is get them to decide that what they're doing is wrong.'

What if I can't talk my boss round?

'Sometimes you need to accept that decisions are made that aren't the ones you'd make,' says Ms Kennett. 'If you're quite senior, you may well be expected to implement decisions you disagree with, otherwise you'll be seen as not holding the line.'

In other circumstances, Mr Redman warns against giving ultimatums or making threats. 'You don't want to escalate the conflict,' he says. 'You should be assertive – which isn't the same as being arrogant or forceful.'

Ms Kennett adds: 'You may have some recourse to your boss's boss. But you need to be very careful here. You don't want to ruin your relationship with your boss.'

Should I formally note my disagreement?

It depends. 'If it needs to go on the record, use your political skills and organizational awareness,' says Mr Redman. 'There are often far more sophisticated ways of ensuring your stance is known – such as knowing the right person in whose ear to have a quiet word – than using formal channels.'

But if you must go on the record, Ms Kennet advises: 'You need to write something like "I strongly advise against this. But I'll support you in it."'

Working with difficult colleagues

At some point in their career, most people will have to work with someone obstructive, difficult and generally unpleasant. So, how do you deal with the jerks at work?

Is it just you?

'Try to discover whether this person is unpleasant to you or generally like this,' advises executive coach Miranda Kennett. 'Misery loves company, so just swapping notes can really mitigate the nastiness of it... You might also find that there are particular times this person is unpleasant or certain triggers.'

On the other hand, if it is just you, then you are likely to be dealing with a bully. 'Bullies pick on people who cave in easily,' says Ms Kennett. 'So stand up to them. Don't be aggressive but be firm. Don't give them the reaction they want.'

How do I fight back?

Sometimes telling people they're being unpleasant is enough. 'Some people have a remarkable lack of self-awareness,' says Robert Sutton, professor of management science and engineering at Stanford University and author of *The No Asshole Rule: Building a Civilized Workplace and Surviving One That Isn't.* 'When you confront them they often can't believe they've been like that.'

Whenever you challenge people, what you say should be rooted in examples and deal with facts. 'Be very specific,' says Ms Kennett. 'Being generic weakens your case. Also frame it along the lines of: "I feel very angry about the way you attacked me in front of the client." That way they can't say you're wrong.'

Professor Sutton adds you may have to document evidence of their unreasonable behaviour to make a case to HR or their boss. This is far more persuasive if done as a team: 'If one person does this they're crazy. But if three of you do, it's a movement.'

How do I cope?

There are situations in which your abilities to fight back will be limited. 'If it's your boss, you may have to find a strategy that works with them,' suggests Cary Cooper, professor of organizational psychology at Lancaster University. 'Figure out a way to understand what they psychologically need... In a funny sort of way, it can become a game.'

Ms Kennett warns against becoming obsessed with the situation. 'That puts you in victim mode, saps your energy and means the nasty person has won. They say it takes two to make a victim.'

It is also worth trying to mentally 'reframe' working for someone unpleasant as a learning experience; that way you feel you are getting something out of it.

What if it is a colleague or a subordinate?

Bullying often comes from a small distance above. But if they are a colleague, some of the same advice applies, with the caveat that it may be easier to ignore or isolate them and try and work around them. With subordinates, the obvious answer is to fire them. But Professor Sutton notes that this can be difficult if they are highly regarded. 'In this case, you should at least make them aware of the effect their behaviour is having on other people. Some people can and do learn.' Ultimately, though, you may have to ask yourself if even a very talented person is worth keeping if they act as a drag on everyone else.

At what point should I consider my position?

You need to be pragmatic – developing a thicker skin is no bad thing. 'You don't choose your colleagues and whenever people work together there will be conflict,' notes Professor Cooper. But, equally, you should recognize that there are some situations and people you cannot change.

Being the bearer of bad news

No one likes breaking bad news to staff. But doing it well helps to minimize the fallout, limit morale problems and protect your employer brand. So how do you tell people what they do not want to hear?

How can I prepare the ground?

Bad news should not come as a total surprise. 'Ideally you should start making the case beforehand,' says David Ferrabee, managing director of Able and How, a change communications consultancy.

Where possible, people should be kept up to speed about what is happening even before any final decisions are made. 'If the company is in bad financial shape, your staff should know,' says Cary Cooper, professor of organizational psychology at Lancaster University School of Management. 'Be direct and say, "We are in a lot of trouble and if we don't make changes we could go down."'

Are there different kinds of bad news?

Yes, says Professor Cooper. 'There's individual bad news and bad news for a group or the entire organization. Each requires a different approach.' Of course, there's also a whole spectrum of bad news from the trivial (no more free biscuits) to the very serious (a 20 per cent headcount reduction).

How do I break bad news to a group of people?

Usually this is easier as individuals are unlikely to feel singled out. The best approach, Mr Ferrabee says, is to humanize the news and be straight. 'Tell people things as truthfully and as clearly as you can. Avoid jargon and tell them who will be affected… Admit everything as long as you don't open yourself up to lawsuits. It's good to push legal people on what you can say,' he says.

You should also allow time for the news to sink in, he says. 'Remember that, as a manager, you have known for some time and have had time to deal with it,' he adds.

Professor Cooper says it can help to involve those affected. 'Managers often think the best way is to impose change. But if you involve staff, they feel a sense of ownership. So instead of saying "Here is how we're making 15 per cent savings," say: "We need to save 15 per cent. Does anyone have any suggestions?"'

How do I deliver bad news to an individual?

This can be harder, especially if you are making someone redundant. Mr Ferrabee says people are often quite brutal when announcing job losses – largely because making someone redundant is horrible and they do it clumsily. Again, he says, you need to set out the case, 'Tell the person the reasons behind it, how the process works and what sort of safety net the company provides.'

But while some are too direct, others equivocate. 'You have to be clear,' says Miranda Kennett, an executive coach. 'The person needs to understand what has happened.'

More generally, she says that if people react badly to individual bad news of any type, you should allow them to. The classic first response to bad news is denial.

What is unacceptable?

For serious bad news, you must deliver it face to face and as soon as possible. 'Hearing from a third party or reading about it in a newspaper isn't good and damages your employer brand,' says Ms Kennett. 'Texting or e-mailing is completely unacceptable. Be brave and face up to it.'

Professor Cooper adds that you should not try to muddy the waters either. 'If it's news like a merger, don't lie about job cuts. Mergers and acquisitions never create jobs. Say, "People may have to go and we'll tell you as soon as we know."'

Working for a bad boss

The adage 'People don't leave companies, they leave bosses' has a lot of truth to it. But with new jobs hard to come by, many people have to make the best of working for a bad boss.

What kinds of bad bosses are there?

Incompetent bosses are the most common, but in some respects clueless bosses are fairly innocuous. 'With an incompetent boss, you can ultimately empower yourself to compensate for your boss's failings,' says Jane Clarke of business psychologists Nicholson McBride.

However, John Hoover, author of *How to Work for an Idiot*, points out that you should not do so at the expense of your own career: 'If you abdicate all power and responsibility to someone less talented and intelligent than you, then who is the idiot?'

Far worse, however, are bosses who are Machiavellian, paranoid, sadistic or even masochistic. 'If your boss is a Machiavelli, you need to learn what drives them,' says Mr Hoover. 'Present yourself as value added to what they want to achieve. This doesn't mean you compromise who you are, but it does mean you don't inadvertently get in their way. Do that and they'll rip your heart out and say it's nothing personal. Learn who you're dealing with and don't inhibit their career ambitions.'

He adds that similar strategies work with other dysfunctional managers. 'With sadistic bosses, you need to fake your suffering. Give an impression of being under tremendous pressure while getting the work done. With a masochistic boss, you need to be part of their disaster and offer sympathetic comments. Ensure you all appear to suffer together.'

How bad is bad?

Ask yourself if your boss really is that terrible. 'Sometimes it's just a personality difference,' says executive coach Geraldine Gallacher. 'Introverts often find extroverts insufferable and you might think your boss very insensitive but then discover that you can say whatever you like to them.'

Ms Clarke adds: 'If your boss is technically competent but lacks emotional intelligence, you may be able to work around that.'

Are there any general coping strategies?

'Shrink them in your mind. Don't dwell on them and feel resentful, and don't allow yourself to indulge in endless boss-bashing or analysis of their behaviour,' says Ms Gallacher. 'Try to get some perspective.

While the boss looms large in your imagination, it's unlikely you loom large in theirs. These incidents that trouble you so much may not even register with them.'

Ms Clarke advises putting some strategic distance between yourself and your boss: 'Forge strong relationships with other stakeholders and ensure they know you're doing a good job.'

Should I take a stand?

'A lot of people think they'll be honoured for taking on a bad boss, but you should remember that the organization gave power to the bad boss in the first place,' advises Mr Hoover. 'When you challenge a bad boss, you're making demands on senior executives to act and they'd rather not.'

That said, there is often a tipping point when the time to strike is right, but you need to be politically savvy enough to recognize it. 'Getting away with murder in an organization depends on how many other people want the victim dead.'

Are there any upsides?

Some people say they learn more from bad bosses than good ones. In addition, Mr Hoover notes how a bad boss can present opportunities to bolster your standing if your ability to cope with them is recognized. 'You want to be known as someone who deals skilfully with difficult people,' he says.

Ms Gallacher adds, 'It's a real chance to practise your influencing skills,'

How to make cuts

With the economy still tough, many managers are wondering when they will next have to wield the knife. So how do you ensure you cut like a surgeon, not a butcher?

How should I approach cuts?

'Face the truth and act early,' says Alex Pratt, author of *Austerity Business*. 'If something is not right, the longer you leave it the worse it gets. When the business environment changes, you've got to refit your ship to be fit for purpose.'

He adds that the pain should not be delivered in stages: 'Do it once and cut deep. Don't slice slivers away, month after month. That can be very demoralizing.'

Ian Gooden, chief operating officer of human resources consultancy Chiumento, says: 'Deciding what to cut can be very difficult. Know what motivates your team and cut in the right places. Social people might prefer to take a 10 per cent pay cut and not lose colleagues, whereas materialistic people might feel very differently.'

You may also be better off focusing cuts – for example, losing an entire team or unit instead of spreading the pain across the whole business. Budgetary cuts are easier than people cuts – but be straightforward and do not use them as a way of trying to force people out.

How do I cut?

'The big challenge is choosing which people you let go and which you keep,' says Mr Gooden. 'Managers who haven't done this before often really struggle. They can't help but see them as people, but you need to stay objective. If you're not, there could be legal challenges.'

David Ferrabee, managing director of change communications consultancy Able and How, says: 'You need to tell people in a coherent and humanistic way. You should set up meetings where people are informed of the process that's going to start. You do hear of catastrophes such as people realizing they've been sacked when their car park pass doesn't work. It's really about managers stepping up and being honest, decent and sensitive. Tell the people who are affected first and then tell the rest.'

Mr Gooden says all those involved in the process need to be consistent in their message so as not to cause confusion or give false hope or despair. 'Disconnects can turn the gas up under an already difficult situation.' He adds: 'Some managers try and distance themselves by saying: "I'm just the messenger." This is not the case – here, you are the organization's representative.'

What should I avoid?

Mr Pratt says that people often look at what is easiest to cut rather than what is best. 'Two things that can get cut very quickly are marketing spend and training because of their impact on cash flow. But the people you need in a downturn are your customers and your team.'

Trivial savings may not be worthwhile either. 'The classic is cutting free tea and coffee in the office but this creates disproportionate fear and hacks people off,' he adds.

Try to avoid insensitive coincidences, such as cuts for some followed by bonuses for others, says Mr Ferrabee. 'Feel people's pain, but don't make hollow attempts at empathy,' he says.

What about the aftermath?

People tend to worry about those who have been cut, but as a manager, those who haven't are of more concern to you.

'Those who stay will experience a short-term rebound,' says Mr Gooden. 'But in the longer term they'll realize it's harder and benefits have fallen. You need to ensure productivity doesn't fall and you need to re-establish trust. You have to say, "I told you what I had to do and I did it." It may not be pleasant.'

Are cuts all bad?

'A bad economy often reveals problems that you haven't seen before whereas a good one masks them,' says Mr Pratt. Mr Gooden adds, 'Sometimes cuts force you to take action and the result is better than what was there before. Sometimes you need that pressure.'

How to handle a bad appraisal

No one enjoys a bad appraisal. But how should you react if you receive one? And what can you do if you think it is unfair?

How should I respond when my manager starts to deliver the bad news?

'The most important thing is not to overreact,' says Bobbie LaPorte, a San Francisco-based career coach. 'Don't get defensive and don't respond emotionally. If you think it is undeserved, listen and take notes.'

Try to get a written copy and take time to consider your next move. She adds. 'Say, "I'm not sure I agree with your conclusions. I'd like an opportunity to pull my thoughts together and come back."'

What should I do next?

Robert Myatt, a director at business psychologists Kaisen, says: 'We always tell managers to provide specific examples and make it clear that these form the basis for the feedback. If the manager is not doing this you need to ask them to do so. This could also push them to find evidence that could refute their conclusions.'

You should also look at whether your performance goals are clear and whether they might have changed over the period because it is very easy for the goals you agreed to drift – especially if you are working remotely. 'It is also worth asking if you have been ignoring the signs during informal performance reviews. Perhaps you need to make these more formal,' says Ms LaPorte.

You should also ask yourself how big a deal this is. Rosemary Smart of human resources consultants Penna says: 'Understand the level of importance of this appraisal. Is it something that could affect promotion or bonuses or is your boss just going through the motions?'

What if I think it is unfair?

'You must let your manager know,' says Ms Smart. 'They may say "You're right, I was a bit harsh. Perhaps I got it wrong." Lots of managers have no training in this area, and have to do 20–30 people. They may have had a bad day or you may have got into an adversarial situation.'

You may also have taken minor criticism to heart. But equally managers sometimes do mark people down for very bad reasons. If you believe this is the case and your manager refuses to budge, explain that you are going to lodge a grievance complaint in order to resolve matters; most organizations will have an HR process to deal with this situation.

What if there is merit in it?

'Get clarity in terms of the specific behaviours that are seen as negative,' says Mr Myatt. 'Managers shouldn't just cite examples, they should show a pattern. Getting to the root causes of the underperformance is the most useful thing you can do and the key to avoiding it in the future.'

You then need to plan positively to change things. Ms LaPorte says, 'Ask your manager, "How can we work together? How can you help me? What do I need to do differently?" Discuss goals and have them put in writing. Then ask for regular opportunities to discuss your progress, ideally once a quarter. You may have to take the initiative here – managers often don't like doing reviews.'

Mr Myatt says that developing self-awareness can avoid future problems, 'Try to understand who you are. If the pattern of underperformance is very pronounced you might not be playing to your strengths. You may need to change your environment or even your job.'

Dealing with calls for your resignation

Calls for you to resign can come from fellow board directors, your line manager, your colleagues, dissident shareholders or media pundits. How should you respond to calls for you to fall on your sword?

How serious are they?

You need to ask where these calls are coming from. If they're from your fellow board directors or immediate colleagues, that's pretty serious; if they're from a few dissident shareholders or a media pundit, less so. 'It is a bit like feedback,' says Elisabeth Marx, a partner at Stonehaven, an executive recruitment company. 'If it's one or two voices, it might not matter. But if all your stakeholders are aligned, you had better take it seriously.'

Rod Clayton, corporate issues specialist at PR group Weber Shandwick, says you need to be sure you are not being unfairly maligned. 'Even if you feel the request merits consideration, it's unlikely that you should accede to it immediately,' he says. 'You may be being picked out or set up. Or the people calling for your resignation may not know the whole picture.'

It is, therefore, important to take advice from someone who can give you a cool, objective view.

Don't let others control the narrative

'Perception is really important,' says Graham Abbey, an executive coach at March Friday. 'You might think it is all nonsense and that you don't want to lend these voices credibility by acknowledging them. But often you need to manage the conversations people have about you as they do affect how others see you.'

Mr Clayton adds: 'You don't want to get into a situation where the noise around the calls for your resignation means the organization cannot operate effectively with you there.'

The difficulty, says Mr Abbey, is that you may not be able to use all the facts publicly for reasons such as commercial confidentiality. 'It can often be about telling a story that people believe that counters the calls for you to go.'

If you are in a senior role, there is always likely to be interest and you should keep a cool head, as anger will play into the hands of your detractors and may damage you in the court of public opinion.

What can I say to those calling on me to resign?

'Often it is simply a case of convincing people that in the long term you'll be worth it,' says Mr Clayton. 'Short-termism can be a real problem – in business, sports and politics. But any sensible stakeholder will usually listen to a rational case.'

Calls to resign from fellow board directors are likely to be very serious. 'It won't be something they do lightly,' says Ms Marx. But if you are below board level, she says the first port of call should be your HR director. 'They're usually very good at managing these situations and can find out what the reasons are and whether they're justified or if it's a malicious campaign.'

If it is public anger, Mr Abbey says you should restate the world as you see it. 'You should seek to weather the storm, but you still need to be wary of the effects on your reputation.'

If you do survive, you should try to make peace with those who wanted you to go – within reason.

There are situations when you should take the advice

'Sometimes it can be the right thing to do,' says Mr Abbey. 'You can say, "I'm going to take a career hit now" with a view to the long term. A resignation can often stop an unfolding story in its tracks and even improve your reputation.'

'Resignation can sometimes be the right course of action for both the individual and the organization,' says Mr Clayton.

A career-limiting move

Whether a monumental professional mistake or a huge and public personal embarrassment, a career-limiting move is something that so undermines you, it is hard to imagine recovering from it. But are all occupational and reputational disasters as bad as they seem?

What should my first move be?

Get some perspective. 'It can feel like the end of the world when you're in the eye of the storm,' says Phil Hall, chairman of the PR agency PHA Media and a former *News of the World* editor. 'But things usually move on pretty quickly. It's often only of passing interest to other people.'

Jo Ellen Grzyb, a psychotherapist and co-founder of Impact Factory, a personal development company, says: 'Think of it as a problem to be solved, rather than a reason to panic. Say: "I've got into this mess, now what do I do?" Do this immediately rather than hope it'll go away.'

How can I repair my reputation?

Mr Hall says: 'Accept the mistake, say you're sorry and take responsibility. Don't try to cover it up. People accept mistakes but they won't accept a cover-up. Do this and move on.'

Peter Shaw, author of *Thriving in Your Work*, says you should demonstrate that you have learnt something. 'Say: "We all learn more from our mistakes than our successes." Be truthful and measured in what you say and don't sound or look panicked. If it was a bad decision you made, be willing to explain the thinking that led to the decision.'

You should also ensure your supporters are fully briefed. 'In any organization there are key people who make or break reputations,' says Mr Shaw. 'Be sure you explain to your champions what happened. They can speak up for you.'

You should also remember that the best way of getting people to forget about your failures is to bury them in successes so they become ancient history. 'Look at footballers,' Mr Hall says. 'If they screw up, the best form of PR for them is to win matches.'

Is humiliation different?

A career-limiting move such as making a fool of yourself at an office party differs because it is not about your ability to do your job. Ms Grzyb says: 'Put on a bold face and take it on the chin rather than pretend it didn't happen. There's something to be said for admitting what you did and throwing yourself at the mercy of the court. You can also pre-empt the mutterings that you'll hear by saying to people: "I'm sure you've heard of me." This way, people know you know and that you're dealing with the crisis.'

Mr Hall says: 'People will often feel sympathy for you. They realize that everyone has skeletons in the cupboard. So be apologetic and have a sense of humour; make jokes at your own expense. It doesn't make you bad at what you do.'

Are there any upsides?

'A bit of notoriety could make you stand out from the crowd,' Mr Hall says.

Indeed, some larger-than-life characters seem to thrive on disasters that would fell lesser mortals. Recovering from a calamity can give you a memorable personal narrative – and people love stories.

Working for a company that's in disgrace

Having your employer publicly dragged through the mud is unpleasant and can affect your life both in and outside the office. How do you cope with working for public enemy number one?

How bad is it?

'The main thing is context,' says Helen Wright of research and consulting firm Great Place to Work. 'There is a world of difference between a company which conducts itself well having a bad PR moment and one where the culture is deeply problematic.'

Jessica Pryce-Jones, CEO of iOpener, a workplace happiness and performance consultancy, adds that you need a sense of proportion. 'It may help to remember that there are shysters everywhere. It just so happens you work for a business that is in the spotlight at the moment – and it will probably blow over.'

What difficulties am I likely to encounter?

'Work is part of who we are and we like to have a connection to what we do,' says business psychologist Jean Roberts. 'If you lack this, cognitive dissonance can become a problem.'

Philippa Foster Back, director of the Institute of Business Ethics at Oxford University's Saïd Business School, notes: 'At an individual level you have your personal values, then societal values and corporate values. If there's tension between these and you're being asked to compromise your personal values, you may become stressed and anxious.'

What can I do?

If it is a relatively short-term problem, you may just be able to take it on the chin. However, cynical detachment isn't much good in the long run. 'Leaders need to get people talking and create forums where this can happen,' says Ms Foster Back.

Ms Roberts adds: 'Become an influencer: find like-minded people and tell those above what you're not comfortable with. Even lowly employees can champion change.'

Taking action will go a long way towards making you feel better, but there are quick fixes too. 'Sit down and list your options – up to and including venting on Twitter and even full whistle-blowing,' says Ms Pryce-Jones. 'You probably shouldn't actually do these things, but knowing you have options helps you regain a sense of control.'

How do I deal with it outside work?

A few snide comments are not going to hurt but there's only so much laughing it off you can do. 'You might say, "I don't know all the details – I was shocked and surprised," ' says Ms Foster Back. 'It is about recognizing it and not being in denial.'

What happens if I go elsewhere?

'Getting another job may be a problem if you're very senior,' says Ms Foster Back. 'But if you're in the middle you should be prepared to be asked to give your views on it.'

But avoid criticizing your previous employer overtly, as this comes across as unprofessional.

'People learn through bad experiences,' says Ms Wright. 'So whilst it may be unpleasant at the time it can be good CV fodder.'

Coping with idea thieves

Having others take the credit for your work is infuriating and feels deeply unfair. How can you deal with those who appropriate your ideas?

Take early action

'Be as pre-emptive as possible,' says Nancy Ancowitz, a business communication coach and author of *Self-Promotion for Introverts*. 'You tend to know who the scene-stealers are. So make sure your boss sees who is doing the work. Talk about what you're doing and send e-mails saying things like: "I have this idea for cost-cutting and I'll present it in Monday's meeting." '

She suggests bringing hard copies of documents you've written about the idea to meetings. 'There's nothing like your ideas in print to reinforce whose brainchild they are.'

Mike Phipps, author of *21 Dirty Tricks at Work: How to Win at Office Politics*, adds: 'Seek input from others on your work. Say: "I'd like your thoughts on this." The single biggest piece of insurance is having allies in that meeting who know it was your idea.'

What do I do after it happens?

Ceri Roderick of business psychologists Pearn Kandola says: 'Someone appropriating your work triggers strong feelings. This is why you need to manage your visceral response. Be measured and calm.'

Mr Roderick adds: 'You should interrogate yourself. Ask if you're overreacting – sometimes you will need to let it go.'

For lesser incidents and one-offs, a low-level response may be appropriate. 'You should have a quiet word with the person as they may not have thought, or they could be careless,' says Mr Roderick.

Mr Phipps adds that 'if it's more important, you may choose to go for more of an intervention, where you regain ownership of the idea or work. Here you need proof. When you get the evidence, speak to the person face to face. This signals assertion, self-confidence and professionalism.

'If you do it in person, you are much more likely to have a productive conversation. But allow the other person to save face – and offer a resolution that will work for them. You might say: "I noticed this report now has your name on it, not mine. Someone must have made a mistake when they were printing it." This is important: if you corner a rat in a garden shed, it will fight, but if you show it the door and sunlight, it will take the easy way out. A rat always does.'

Telling everyone your work was stolen runs the risk of you looking childish.

What if it is my boss?

'If you show a report to your manager,' says Mr Phipps, 'that you know will be presented to the board and they say, "Great, I'll take it from here," you might ask: "But how will you deal with the difficult questions?"'

However, Ms Ancowitz says that 'you may have to accept it. It is part of your job to make the boss look good and you can't expect credit for every minor contribution. You might also ask yourself if you see your contribution reflected in your pay or bonus – that could make it okay.'

Dealing with a major falling out

After a disagreement you and a co-worker could be on such bad terms that you may not even be speaking. Can you repair the damage – and what avenues are open to you?

How important is the relationship?

'One option is to ask whether you can get by without that relationship,' says Graham Abbey, an executive coach at March Friday. 'You don't have to be best buddies with everyone at work.' However, he adds, if it is a meaningful relationship that influences you, you will need to deal with it and take some responsibility.

How do I approach the person?

'You could try the non-violent communications model,' says Mike Leibling, author of *Working with the Enemy: How to survive and thrive with really difficult people*. 'State what you've noticed (we're not speaking). Say what you're feeling (it is upsetting me). Tell them what you want (to repair the relationship). And ask a question (What needs to happen for us to get along?). It works well because it's very hard to argue with.'

Alan Redman, a business psychologist at the Criterion Partnership, says: 'You should ask yourself if it's a "thinking" falling out or a "feeling" falling out. With the latter, you might just try a very different approach like being unconditionally positive. Smile often and make eye contact. Give the person positive strokes. Treat it as a very different relationship.

'If it's a thinking falling out, look for points you can agree on and avoid those you don't.'

Mr Redman says that it is actually very hard to rebuff a sincere approach. 'We're social animals and we're wired to respond like for like,' he explains.

Mr Leibling adds that you should not expect perfection, but a good enough relationship is often good enough. 'Ask questions like

"What can I do to ensure this doesn't happen again?" and "Can we try and find a different way forward?"'

What if I am in the right?

Galling as it may seem, you will have to be the bigger person here. However, you should remember that even if the other person has overreacted, these things are rarely completely black and white. 'Recognize that you may have a very different conflict style to them,' says Mr Abbey. 'Bear in mind too that a major falling out very rarely has a single cause.'

Mr Leibling believes that some people just have a very low threshold but that it is better to try to work with them, within reason. 'You have to allow the person to save face as they're not going to admit that you're right. A lot of people do see being reasonable as a weakness,' he says.

What if they won't accept an apology?

Mr Leibling advises: 'You might say, "I'll ask you when you're not angry. I'm looking for a constructive response."'

Mr Abbey adds: 'If you're rebuffed continually, you may have to say, "I did everything I could. I need to find a way to work with the relationship as it is."'